‹CODE YOUR WAY UP›

GREG THOMAS

CODE
YOUR
WAY UP

Rise to the Challenge
of Software Leadership

JUMPING JIVE PRESS

Cataloguing in publication information is available from Library and Archives Canada.
ISBN 978-1-7770765-0-4 (paperback)
978-1-7770765-1-1 (ebook)

Jumping Jive Press

Produced by Page Two
www.pagetwo.com

Cover design by Jennifer Lum
Interior design by Jennifer Lum
www.codeyourwayup.com

To the chief,
who has never stopped believing in me.

To the girls,
the best team in the world.

‹Contents›

INTRODUCTION

‹If It Were Easy, Everyone Would Be Doing It›

I've always loved to code.

In my second year of business studies at university (way back in 1996), I was up late one night working on a Power-Point presentation about a factory trip our group had recently taken. (Pretty mundane stuff.) It just so happened that one of my roommates was up around the same time working on a project, coding some HTML. I bore witness to what he typed into Notepad and what he displayed in a browser, and I was blown away by the possibilities. I realized what he was doing and what could come from it.

I was hooked.

That night I tossed PowerPoint out the window and wrote my first HTML pages with photos from our factory trip, added some back and forth arrows into the page for good measure, ran it in Internet Explorer and shipped my first code. (If all you took from this is that I used Internet Explorer for a presentation, please hear me out.)

By the end of it all, I cared more about my hard-coded HTML masterpiece than I did about the presentation that I had spent the last few weeks sweating over. I was downright giddy every time I had to click *next* and occasionally clicked *back* when the conversation required it. (I didn't need it ... I wanted to show off.)

Out of a class of fifty business students, not one cared about how I had created my presentation. It wasn't until the very end, after all the "important" questions were asked, that my professor asked how I did it.

One person liked what I did.

One person.

Not the person or people whom I was trying to connect with (and maybe educate), but someone liked it.

Good enough for me!

From that experience, I realized two things:

1   I wanted to code for the rest of my life.
2   It's essential to know whom you are coding for.

Like any newbie, I consumed every book about coding I could get my hands on as fast as possible. During those formative years, I read coding books, blogs, articles and nothing else. If it didn't have anything to do with coding, I wasn't reading it.

The next eight years were spent cranking out code mornings, evenings and weekends; cursing myself for choosing bad libraries; drinking way too much caffeine; and altogether making the most of the opportunity to develop some incredible products and projects. In short, these were what I like to call the wonder years, when everything was new and everything was possible. Just when I thought I was reaching the apex of my career, I was asked to lead a new team composed of some of the smartest people I had ever worked with. Up until this point, the only person I had led in anything was me, and, to my surprise (shock, dismay), there was no manual or onboarding session to get me up to speed and show me the path.

Sure, I'd done the odd stint as a technical or project lead and run with ideas with the help of other people. I'd done the token trip to New York to win over a customer for the company I was working for, but that was about as far as my leadership experience went.

I knew the difference between the good, the bad and the ugly of leadership. I had ideas about what I would do if I ever had the opportunity to lead a team—and now here it was. I'd like to say I started the first day with a well-defined plan for what everyone was going to do, how we would accomplish our objectives, how they would meet their career goals and how I would keep leveling up my coding game.

I didn't.

Even after settling into the role, I still made mistakes. As an "instaLeader," I was now responsible for a lot more than my own career; I was responsible for everyone on my team as well. (Who knew?) And amidst all this learning, I still had to deliver code—and not only my own. If you've never had to be responsible for someone else's code, let me tell you, it's a whole new ball game and it gives rise to emotions you never thought existed within you. At each design or code review, conflicting thoughts were always running through my head:

> *How do I tell them this is bad?*

> *This is amazing; I can see what they're trying to do. But it's going to take forever to finish.*

> *OMG, this is so good. Why can't I be as good a coder as they are?*

Like I said, emotions.

Leadership is an overwhelming endeavor.

If it were easy, everyone would be doing it.

But that doesn't mean you shouldn't try. For years I have heard people say, "I'm not a leader. I'm not good with people." Or "I'm a better coder than I am a leader." And all I can think is, *Someone once sold you that line and you bought it—hook, line and sinker.*

During my first year as a software manager, I was constantly whispering (actually full-on muttering) to myself:

> ➤ "I wish I had started doing some of this work when I was learning to code."

> ➤ "Why did I hold back in those discussions?"

> ➤ "I should have jumped in on those other opportunities a bit more."

> ➤ "For crap's sake, Greg, get it together and focus."
> (That last one was used the most.)

Through those good, bad and ugly days, I learned that anyone can lead, but leadership starts with treating it with as much love, dedication and willingness to fail as you do your own code.

Why are you waiting for someone to tell you to lead?

Who's stopping you from taking the initiative and jumping in?

Who decided your growth and development were no longer your responsibility?

After years of leading projects and teams, the big secret I've learned about being a great leader in software is to never forget the code. Not *to* code, but *the* code. Coding and leading at the same time is your secret weapon. When you start treating them as silos and thinking, *Today I'll do this, tomorrow I'll do that, next week will be a people week and this week will be a code week,* that's when things start to go sideways and you lose control of what you have to offer.

The absolute best part about coding (no software developer will ever disagree with this) is that moment when it all works, when it all comes together, that swell of euphoria and adrenaline that pumps through your veins symbolizing that you have accomplished what you thought was impossible. We all know that feeling, we've all had it; everything clicks into place and we forget about all the sweat and tears that went into getting it to work and we willingly go back to the well for more.

Maybe you've just created your first console/web/cloud Hello World masterpiece in all its hard-coded glory and you're starting to have thoughts about working with others, building a start-up or leading a team, like I did. Or maybe you've been recently thrown off the cliff to see if you can fly (which is a much harder situation than being thrown into the ocean to see if you can swim).

You can get the same euphoric feeling leading people and teams, and, yes, it all starts with code.

1

GETTING STARTED

etting Started guides are a peek into what can be accomplished *after* you have set everything up correctly. As a developer, I've never read one in my entire life. I've always stumbled through the problem, learning more as I go.

This chapter is that guide, so don't be like me—please read this Getting Started.

When I was editing this chapter, StackOverflow released their 2019 Developer Survey results (https://insights.stackoverflow.com/survey/2019). In it, there were no questions about leadership or growth. Perhaps that wasn't the focus of the survey, but maybe that's the problem.

I've always thought of leadership as being akin to a race condition. Wikipedia's exquisite definition of *race condition* is as follows:

> A race condition or race hazard is the behavior of an electronics, software or other system where the system's substantive behavior is dependent on the sequence or timing of other uncontrollable events. It becomes a bug when one or more of the possible behaviors is undesirable.

It's that last bit—*one or more of the possible behaviors is undesirable*—that's the key to coding leadership.

You are always going to have days and weeks when you will prioritize one of those possible behaviors over another, but to be a success, you can never *not* do one of those behaviors every single day of your career. From the moment you get dressed for your first day of your first job to the moment when you turn in your keyboard, what you achieve is rooted in your approach to these behaviors.

This book isn't about how you should code, what syntax to use, which languages are best etc., etc. This book is about how to take all that incredible knowledge and bundle it into a set of skills you never thought you had. Skills that will make you successful at whatever role you take on.

These skills and behaviors are sometimes referred to as *soft skills*—I don't know why. They are tough skills to learn and even harder to master, and they come with such a conflux of emotions that I would call them anything but soft. I don't want you to make these skills part of your repertoire so you have one more entry you can add to LinkedIn. I want you to embed them into everything you do. Only then will they stop being "soft" skills and start being the behaviors that you need.

Careers in software development change at an exponential rate, propelled by the pace of innovation and the people who can deliver it. You can come from any background, take any set of courses in high school, college, university or elsewhere, and still be able to find a career that works for your life.

You can code the nights away trying to figure out what works and what doesn't until you discover what you like, and then you can keep building on that as a foundation.

And if you get bored along the way?

You can change the parameters, switch from being a front-end to a back-end developer to focusing on databases first and everything else last.

The paths are endless.

If you're still not sure that this book is for you (because of some preconceived notions about the current role you are in), here are the people who have been front and center in my mind while I've been writing this book:

You: The recent graduate who took an amazing coding course that sparked something deep within you. Now you are ready to embark on a career path in one of the most interesting fields ever, where the roads are endless and opportunities abound.

You: The tinkerer who stays up late into the night, drifting into the early morning, trying to understand not just how but also why something works. And not because you are being paid to do it but because not knowing eats away at you day and night as you try to solve the problem.

You: The architect who sees the world through a different lens, struggling with how to convey your vision not only in creating something new but in trying to push the boundaries of how and what you deliver.

You: The developer who's been thrown off the cliff by last-minute production bugs for months and is now being given the reins to figure out a way to permanently stop the bleeding.

You: The team lead who is trying to break out of the monotonous pattern of ensuring all their tests pass and recognizing that the barometer of success has changed and they need to change with it.

You: The software manager who made that slick transition from developer to team lead but now struggles with a new set of responsibilities that have no relation to what you always thought was your hallmark skill set—coding like mad until your keyboard sang with delight.

Or maybe you are some combination or permutation of these personas, and you're on a completely different path.

Or you might not have had that hard talk with the mirror yet, but you know that now is the time to sort things out.

It's for all of you.

‹How It Works›

I'm a big proponent of visualizations and drawing things out. To get started, we are going to focus on the following behaviors as they pertain to development: drive, initiative, leadership, delivery and growth.

This is a very clear, concise display of what behaviors are important to have when working in software.

You've probably seen something similar before. This diagram has a very human resources feel to it—four perfectly balanced circles that add up to equally perfect growth. If I wanted to be fancy, I would apply some colors to it (with some slick gradients) and it'd be ready for a brochure.

On the surface this seems brilliant: do these four things in equal measure and grow.

But this is not real.

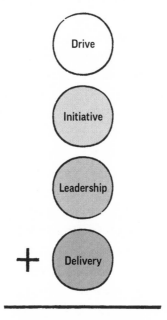

GROWTH

Can I Lose One?

Does this sound familiar? *I like drive, I like initiative and I'm a big fan of delivery, but leading people is not really my thing.*

Or maybe this: *I think maybe I'll leave the leadership stuff to someone else on the team and simply focus on the other three, overcompensating on the delivery side.*

No, you're not going to do that, and whoever has been letting you do that needs to stop. Maybe leading people—as it's written about on blogs and in books—isn't "your thing," but "leading" is everyone's thing. Let me show you.

Is there trouble with a piece of code that you wrote for a customer's site? I highly doubt you're going to sit back and let people struggle with it. No, you're going to jump in, take the lead and help that customer get back on their feet.

Is QA having issues accessing the new features that your team built, but everyone else is dealing with emergency bugs? Looks like you're leading the QA team on a walkthrough of what's in the latest release, how they can test it and what they need to watch out for.

Does the PM not know where to find that new feature you built? Sit down with them to watch where they click on the app so you can see where the gap is as opposed to sending them a screenshot that says "click here."

Look who just became a leader and started saving the day!

The only reason you have these preconceived notions of leadership—what you can and can't do—is because you are already in that box (doesn't matter how you got there) and you can feel it closing in around you. You've been fed so much "feel-good feedback" that you now believe this to be the only truth:

"You're so good at being a tech lead and focusing on how to build the application. Why do you want to worry about the people who build it?"

"You're great at focusing on the team. Leave the solution design and coding to someone else."

"Keep doing what you're doing."

We Are Not the Same

We are all different. We all have different paths we want to follow, different aspirations and goals we want to achieve and different styles for how we want to get there. Someone who is keen on leading a team might put more emphasis on their leadership, communication and team skills from the moment they drop their first line of code. This shows in how they comment, document and present their work to others because that's where their path is taking them. Their colleague who is more concerned with how a product comes together, the underlying platform and communication channels, and how efficiently they move between environments, will focus on those other areas of delivery and leadership and choose to let their work speak for itself.

Both are valid paths to growth. Both individuals are leading and delivering.

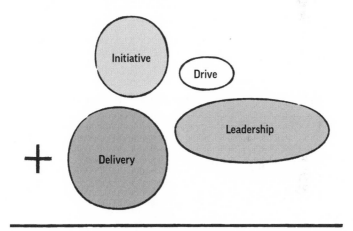

GROWTH

Because people are different, those perfect little circles will expand and contract based on who we are, where our strengths lie, and what our approaches to certain obstacles and opportunities might be. Maybe you have a keen focus on delivery, but you need that swift kick every now and then to shift it into drive?

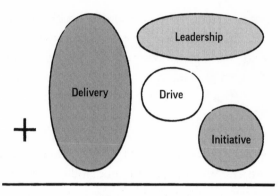

GROWTH

Or maybe this is you?

Or maybe you are somewhere in between. We're all different and we all lean toward different elements that help us grow.

Why Isn't This Adding Up?

No. There is no hard and fast equation to growth; what worked for someone else might not work for you. We are focused on the necessity of having these behaviors that will create growth. Let's tweak the diagram a bit.

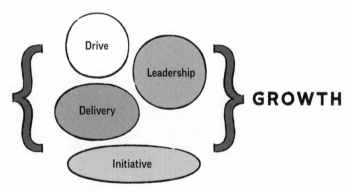

This is an improvement from where we started, but it's still assuming that all these activities are distinct from one another with no overlap between them. Not bad but still not what we are going after.

The Spaces In Between

It has always bothered me that on any growth-and-development diagram all the images are perfectly aligned blocks or circles that line up easily. When I look at them, I always ask the same questions:

> ➤ What's in between them that makes them line up so cleanly and come together so nicely? Is that where all the magic happens?

> ➤ Aren't *taking the initiative* and *leading* a team tied together and overlapping?

> ➤ I can't *deliver* all that incredible code without some *drive*, can I?

> ➤ Can you inspire others to *deliver* when the odds are against you as a *leader* and you don't interface with your team on a daily basis?

The answers to these questions lie in the spaces between the concepts.

These spaces contain uncomfortable emotions—frustration, worry, anxiety, nervousness, confusion and uncertainty. The discomfort prevents us from doing all that we're capable of.

We shy away from giving demos to the team because our code isn't perfect.

We don't share our ideas because we worry how people might respond.

We would rather look at our bug lists than talk with the product owner to figure out the root problem.

The spaces in between are all the behaviors that keep us compartmentalized.

Keeping everything clean is the easy way out.

But these behaviors overlap, and by employing them all at once, we can develop the confidence we need to handle these situations as they arise and get through the worst of it. If we reimagine our diagram, we start to see that our circles begin to overlap as we try new approaches and blend the behaviors we've learned from being a developer into other areas of our growth. As you can see, no behavior covers another completely, and that's good. We can't excel at everything; there is always work to be done (that's the goal).

It's through the overlapping that real growth starts to happen and where the fun starts.

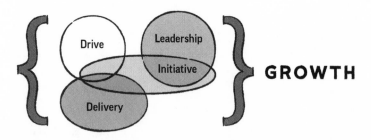

Still Looks Pretty Straightforward

This diagram looks pretty nice, right? Something you might see in a business leadership text, on a blog or TV show where everything is a nice, smooth, overlapping circle of success.

As I look at it now, it is still too clean. Ask anyone who has led people or projects and they will scoff at the idea that leadership is a smooth endeavor or that putting in that extra amount of drive will always have perfect results.

The curves of those circles are never that smooth. They are jagged scratches filled with late-night inspiration and squiggles of projects and products that will never see the light of day. They are us—the work, the effort, everything that we put into our career to make it a success.

What you do, how you work, what you deliver—it's never perfect, never clean, never easy, and when you look at it through the rearview mirror as you head toward the next project, you aren't thinking about how pretty it looks but how happy you are that it's done, it's shipped and it's running.

If you were to apply a "real-life" filter to this diagram, this is how it would be reassembled:

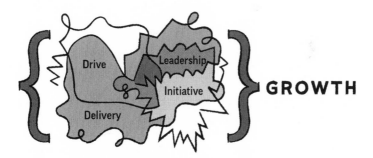

It's a total mess . . . and yet it makes sense. Think about all the ups and downs you've experienced in your career to date. In each case, there was the potential for growth:

"That demo went horribly; does this ever get better?"

"I wish they could see things from my side and all that I'm trying to do."

"Why can't I get this to work?"

If you take a moment, you could probably map events from your own career to this diagram, see what did and didn't work and how all these behaviors start to coalesce.

I can see how being a leader flows into everything I do. I see how my drive pushes me to constantly improve, almost completely overlapping my initiative. I see my delivery—all those jagged marks are the perfect description of the releases I have done over the years—and I see what has worked, what hasn't, what I failed at, what I tried again. And of course, I see all the messiness that went along with every one of those endeavors.

It's never clean and it never will be, because that's what growth is—making mistakes, figuring out what to do better next time and doing it.

‹Sneak Peek›

In each of the following sections of this book, I ask you a set of three questions. These are the hard questions no one (including yourself) is asking you, but they're the questions you need to answer.

1 Where are you stuck? What is holding you back? Who told you to stay where you are? What's driving your frustration?

2 Do you know how to get yourself unstuck? Do you know what options are available to you and what you can do to get out of being stuck? You aren't on one path, are you?

3 Are you ready for what's next? If there was a call to
   action, this question would be it. This is about more than
   getting ready for the next project, the next iteration, the
   next release. This is about going beyond that and asking
   if you're ready for the next role, the next team and the
   next opportunity that is going to come your way.

We'll be discussing each behavior in detail in the coming
pages, but I want to give you a brief synopsis of how I see
each one and how each relates to growth.

Drive

I prefer the word *drive* to *passion*. *Passion* is a great word to
define your interest in something: "I am passionate about
Internet of Things devices. I've bought a kit, played with it,
and even built a small little application—this has been fun."
That shows your passion for IoT.

But when you are driven, when you have a drive for something like the Internet of Things, you start to push yourself to
understand not only how the kit works but also how to make
it better and how to create something that you can productize
and share with the world (or even your circle of friends).

Drive is what keeps you going when the chips are down,
the hours are long and you're feeling burnt out. But you
know the end is near and you refuse to relent. Your learning
and knowledge have gone beyond "oh, that's neat" to reach
"let's do this."

That's growth.

Drive goes beyond code—it has to do with the current project, the team, the customer problems, the vendor

shortcomings, the struggling team member. It's our desire to make something happen and to not relent.

Passion is great, but drive is passion realized.

Initiative

Are you ready to start something?

Are you ready to jump into new opportunities as they present themselves?

When your manager asks for volunteers, are you one of the first few people to raise a hand or do you watch to see what others do?

When the team bug pile gets too big, are you the one who starts chipping away at it to give the final product that little extra bit of polish?

Initiative is summed up by one key question, asked every. single. day: *Can you lead the Army of One?*

Do you have what it takes to lead yourself to do what's next or are you going to watch a movie trailer or a cat video on YouTube?

Will you take the time to teach yourself a new skill, pushing yourself through all those awkward stages of learning, failure and frustration to get there, or will you wait for someone to tell you to do it?

If leadership is about leading others, initiative is about leading one's self. Initiative forms the basis for your own personal growth as it depends solely on what you do.

Initiative is what wakes you up in the morning or keeps you up at night when you need to finish that last online course, compile that last build or fix that bug that's been staring you in the face for days, mocking your every action.

People are often in search of the one characteristic they can employ on the first day to show everyone that they are serious, they are in control and they have what it takes to lead the team. They are looking for a grandiose action that impresses everyone and gets them on board.

What they are looking for is initiative.

Delivery

What you make, what you create, what you share with the world is everything. How you inspire others to do this, how you lead your team on the next release—all these actions are deliverables.

What you deliver will vary over time. It might start off as pure code and perhaps evolve first into coding standards and later into leading your team on a new product launch, but, at the end of it all, it's about delivery.

Delivery is taking something from nothing and creating a thing of value.

Deliveries are our most visible "wins," but they are a double-edged sword and fraught with many pitfalls. We must always be careful to not let things like process, methodology, meetings, extraneous decision-making and other activities become slated as "deliverables."

Attending a meeting *is not* a delivery.

Sending in your status report *is not* a delivery.

Ensuring your team knows when the customer is expecting those last-second, hot-featured fixes and having it in their hands (maybe even a day early) *is* delivery.

Helping your team by taking on the grunt work and reducing their bug piles so you can get the latest release out the door (maybe even a week late) *is* delivery.

The first two examples are busy work; the last two examples are delivery.

Delivery is measured by the value quotient it brings to yourself, your team and your customer.

Leadership

In everything you do, you are a leader.

You might not know it yet or maybe you look at other leaders on your team and think, *That's not me. I can't be like them. They just* know *stuff... sigh.*

You can type *leadership* into Google or Medium and get millions upon millions of results, but it starts at a smaller level: how you interact with your peers and those you take direction from, how you conduct yourself in customer meetings and awkward situations, how you deal with the successes and the failures—all these scenarios are components of leadership and define what kind of leader you can (and will) become.

You don't need a formally structured team to be a leader.

Helping a customer's development team understand the latest coding interface you created *is* leadership.

Working with internal users on user experience testing or demonstrating the new product to sales and marketing *is* leadership.

Troubleshooting problems with a vendor's code (when it's clearly their problem) and not losing your cool *is* leadership.

You are a leader, plain and simple. No *if*s, *and*s, or *but*s. We need your style, your direction, your compass that defines your leadership path, and we need it now.

Growth

When you are executing all four behaviors—not in a time-boxed, sprinted, or componentized way, but concurrently, each and every day, with no concern for when you will get there—you will grow.

Growth is not about adding plus-one years of experience to your LinkedIn profile; it's about looking back and seeing what you've accomplished.

Congrats on moving from senior developer to architect, but did you grow?

Maybe you did, and maybe you didn't. Maybe you thought what you were doing would help you grow and that having a fancy new title would enable that growth, but in the end it didn't.

That's okay. Now it's time to retool your approach.

Growth is paramount to our success. It's what takes a spark of drive and kindles it into something bigger so that when we look back, we say to ourselves, *Wow, I accomplished all of that? That was me? I was on fire.*

When you're on point, you will amaze people with your skill set and they will immediately want you to "keep doing what you are doing" or "focus in on this particular area to become our expert." Be wary of these compliments; if they align with your growth path, fantastic. If they don't or if they aren't accompanied by further direction for your growth and development, then you are being steered down a path created by someone else.

‹Keep Your Head Up›

If you are always working, grinding, delivering, never taking a second to look up and see what is happening around you, you are going to miss some great opportunities.

If you miss some, that's okay, but if you have your head up, you'll see the next ones coming from a mile away, which will give you plenty of time to decide if any are right for you.

One more thing before we really get into it: I want you to write in this book, dog-ear every page, lend it to a friend, make your own diagrams, treat it like a notebook and not a novel. If you're reading this on a tablet or other device, screenshot the segments you like, circle them, put them as your background or on a wall.

That's how you'll remember what's coming next. That's how you'll know what you should be focusing on. That's how you'll grow.

Go ahead and mess it up. Grow with it.

‹Terms of Reference›

Wait, I forgot something.

I'm lazy and tend to use acronyms and make use of terms you may or may not know (or you might not use them in the same way that I do). I've listed all the ones I use in this book on the off chance that you don't know me and have no idea what I'm referring to. For those of you reading this who are not developers (first of all, hello and thank you), hopefully this list helps bring you into the fold.

TERM	WHAT IT IS	WHAT IT MEANS	WHAT IT REALLY MEANS
API	Application Programming Interface	A set of code files that expose functionality to a platform that I can use to access it	I can connect to Facebook and query how many clicks my cat video received.
SDK	Software Development Kit	A collection of APIs (a library) that allows a developer to access and control functions of a platform	Someone much smarter than I am wrote a brilliant interface to a platform that makes my life easier.
UX	User Experience	How the user interacts with the application	What and how they feel when they click on that spinning globe
UI	User Interface	What the user touches or clicks to make things to happen	The action of clicking on my spinning globe
IDE	Interactive Development Environment	The application that you write your code in (yes, NotePad is included here)	The application that makes you constantly wonder how hard it would be to write your own IDE
HOT FEATURE	A critical bug that has morphed into a feature	A bug that was not a bug but instead required the same amount of work as a feature	The customer needs it now because we might have accidentally sold it to them as already being there.

TEAM	WHAT IT IS	WHAT IT MEANS	WHAT IT REALLY MEANS
LIVING DOCUMENT	An incomplete document	A document that everyone keeps adding to over the lifetime of a product or project because not everything was known when we started	A cop-out for those who don't want to finish the document and push the work past when it is required
INSTALEADER	A newly promoted leader	Yesterday you were a developer; today you are a leader and we don't have time to train you.	Buckle up because it's going to be a bumpy ride.
NEWBIE	You being new to anything—a new position, role, project, etc.	You are starting at the ground level and have to learn everything from scratch.	You are constantly creating opportunities to learn, develop and grow.
INTELLISENSE	Prompts that tell us what a function does in code	Directions on where and how to properly use a method and all its overloads	How are you forgetting this again? You've done this one a thousand times at least. Here, in case you forgot (which you did).

If you have your own terms, please email them to me (codeyourwayup@betarover.com). I love learning new things and maybe I'll find somewhere to post them.

2

DRIVE

Growth starts with *drive*—where you want to go, how you want to get there, how far you are going to push yourself and how well you take advantage of every opportunity that comes to you. The blinders are off; you're in a candy store and it's all yours for the taking.

Drive is what gets you hired for the jobs people don't know about yet.

Drive makes you the linchpin of your team.

Drive wakes you up at 4 a.m., as your brain screams with ideas that want to get out.

Drive pushes you through the walls in your path and over those learning humps.

Drive is your passion realized.

Drive throws job titles—junior, intermediate, senior developer—into the trash. I've seen a senior developer who had only two years' experience but also the drive and commitment to rival senior developers with ten years' experience. You don't need to give this kind of person a quiz on syntax and error handling to rank them. They personify drive and most importantly inspire those around them to live and breathe it.

Drive is where we start.

At the core of *drive*, you need to be asking yourself three questions:

1 What keeps me up at night?
2 Can I go the distance?
3 Will I stand out?

Three easy questions to ask that are much harder to answer.

‹What Keeps You Up at Night?›

Ideas keep me up at night, ideas about how I might solve problems—code, people, releases, architecture, anything and everything that I want to put into action the next day.

When I was coding like a madman, I would have dreams about code (and that's when I stopped drinking caffeinated, sugary soda). But as things progressed, those questions that kept me up at night changed. Now I thought about my career, where I was going or how I would handle myself in an interview.

I used to think that my mind had entered this perpetual state of never finishing anything and this was life. What I didn't realize was that my drive was kicking in.

Jobs and Careers Are Different

A job is a task that you perform; you identify the task to be done, you work on it, you complete it and then you move on to the next job. When you're starting out in software, jobs are given out by your manager (which makes sense, since you're still trying to figure out a variety of "Hello World" applications). Jobs are the opportunities that make small deposits in our knowledge bank.

Careers are a collection of jobs, thrown together over our lifetime. Careers are what give you the kick to jump between jobs and to figure out who you want to be, where you want to go and how you want to get there.

Finding Your Paycheck

Getting paid is a sticking point for many (me included) and one that I think is important to discuss early on so we're all on the same page. Yes, you need money to survive, live and have a good life, but the real payoff is what's behind the money, the stuff that keeps you up at night, gazing off into the distance when sitting on the bus or almost veering off the road as you become lost in all its permutations.

The real paycheck is solving cool problems—the truly hard problems that no one wants to work on, the ones everyone shies away from, the ones where there is some convoluted process in place that "cannot be touched because Frank coded it and no one knows what Frank did." That's the paycheck you're after.

Switching careers or taking jobs that offer a lower monetary paycheck but provide greater opportunities for growth is the best way to make an investment in your career that will pay off later in life. Driven leaders know this; that's why they do it.

You are always going to be a newbie (more on this later). You'll always have to learn, always have to recalculate your next destination to get to where you ultimately want to go.

Every company is different, but, from what I have observed, the general rule of thumb is that it takes between two and four months for a newbie to become a contributing member of the team.

Can you bring that number down to three months? Less than two?

Are you going to be able to do that working your standard nine-to-five?

What about Overtime?

This is one of *the* most awkward questions at any interview (and it's always left for the end as you are reaching for your jacket): Do you believe in overtime?

What's the right answer?

"Yes."

"No."

"Four hours is good."

"Twenty-two is too much, but fifteen is just right."

This is a trick question because the interviewer clearly wants you to say, "I love working overtime," so they can check a box. What's important for you is to realize what they are truly asking you.

They aren't asking a question about the overtime *they* need; they are asking how much overtime *you* need to become a valuable part of the team and get out of newbie status.

How committed are *you* to becoming a better *you*?

Do you want to become a valuable, contributing member of their team, someone who gets asked to jump on new projects? (I'm going to venture a yes here.)

Can you do that working the standard nine-to-five? I can't answer for you, but I wasn't able to.

I have always wanted to be a contributing member of my team; I want to finish off my grunt work and get to the challenging projects as quickly as I can. At my first job, I knew I could not do that working the standard nine-to-five. That extra time before nine and after five was the time I needed to learn and grow.

I didn't work sixteen hours a day, Sunday to Sunday, but I did put in extra hours throughout the week, and I did as much grunt work (bugs and emails) as I could during the weekends, so I could clear my schedule for the real work when the rest of the team was online.

It wasn't perfect, but it answered the question—yes, I believed in overtime; how much depended on what I needed to contribute to the team.

I need to be clear here. I am not endorsing a constant stream of overtime with no end goal in mind that personifies the final-crunch mind-set and starts twelve months before you ship. Final crunch is the last month or two (depending on the size of the release). Final crunch is not eight months before you ship, with the date continually being pushed out.

In talking about overtime, I'm talking about how much time you are going to invest in yourself.

ARE YOU MISSING OUT ON THE IMPORTANT LESSONS?

The lessons you need to learn early on are not from training manuals and standards guides. They are from your peers and managers. Approaches to architecture and design, coding discussions, meetings about how to solve problems, figuring out which customers need help this week, and on and on—those are the lessons you want in on.

Reading blogs about architecture, programming books or technical white papers should happen when you go home, on your own time. That's the overtime answer your bosses care about—they want to know how much you are going to invest in yourself.

Do what works for you. Maybe it's setting a goal of learning something new each week. Or maybe you need something more specific like, "I will read relevant articles, blogs or books for six hours a week."

Whatever you decide, write it down and commit to it.

What you choose to learn and what you do with that learning is nobody's responsibility but your own. But don't undermine your learning by missing out on those important lessons that you will only access by being around the office, talking to people about problems, engaging with them and growing.

Driving an Interview

I don't know any developer who has not had at least one sleepless night before an all-important interview for a job that was tailored for them, lining up so perfectly with their experience that it was as if they had been in the room when the job description was being written. Even in that perfect scenario, where we want it so bad, we can still mess it up. (I have.)

Here's what I didn't know. (If I had, it might have let me sleep a little better at night.)

The interview is driven by you, not your interviewer. How long the interview lasts, whether you pique their interest, how you conduct yourself, how you prepare, how much you want it and how many questions they ask—that's all driven by you.

You control the success of the interview; you control the results. There have been times when I did not get the immediate job I was interviewing for, but I did get a call a week later saying, "We were blown away by your interview. You don't have the experience we need for this role, but we have this other thing we want to bring you on for. Are you interested?" That's you controlling the interview.

When I had my first "real" job interview, I was terrified that I wouldn't get the job. I consumed an insane amount of caffeine the week before while learning everything and anything about web development, coding and standards in order to "ace it."

That was my focus—learning the technical stuff, memorizing syntax, running through practice tests, laughing at garbage code I wrote two days before as I learned new skills each and every day.

It was exhausting and whenever I felt myself starting to waver, I kept asking myself one simple question.

Do I Want This Job?

If your answer is any combination of "meh," "not really," "maybe, if this other thing doesn't pan out"—then don't apply. You're wasting everybody's time and energy, including your own. Even if you want the job but not at this company, you should walk away. If you get it, you probably won't take it. The offer they give you will never be enough to entice you to sign on. The paycheck you want and the paycheck you need will never align, which is a good lesson, but you've wasted someone else's time figuring this out.

I don't subscribe to the theory of going to interviews to "practice."

Practice entails doing something on your own time with the goal of getting better. If I go to the ice rink to practice skating, I try some new tricks—some work, some don't, and the ones that do, I save for the big game. The ones that don't, I keep working on, but whatever the result, I'm not wasting someone else's time.

If you want to practice, go find an interviewing coach to help you or ask some friends who have conducted a number of interviews themselves to give you their valuable feedback.

Show up ready to play a game, not a practice.

Be On Time but Not Ahead of Time

Bad weather is not an excuse. Bad weather happens all the time (especially in Canada). Prepare for it. It's a part of life (and it's not going to get any better). If there is bad weather and your car is in the shop and the buses are running slow, grab an Uber or a cab, or call your mom.

Sure, the cost of an Uber or cab ride is forty dollars versus the five dollars you'd spend on public transportation, but is that too much to invest in your career?

What if instead of seeing it as a cost to get there, you see it as the first installment in the investment of your career. If that forty dollars leads to you getting the job of your dreams (as your dreams exist today), is it worth it?

By showing up late to an interview, you've already put the seeds of doubt in the interviewers' mind. You haven't even done anything, they haven't even said hi to you, but you've already given them this view of who you are.

The converse also applies. If you show up ten or fifteen minutes early, that is acceptable and welcome. If you show up forty-five minutes early, that's a little problematic for the people interviewing you. One, they might be interviewing someone else, and two, they most likely have other things on their plates to focus on. Again, you're putting them in an awkward position before they even meet you.

In the event that you do arrive very early, go find a coffee shop, a bench, a chair, something—use that time to review what you are going to say and how you are going to control the conversation.

Do Your Homework

Invariably, the interviewer will ask the first gatekeeping question: "Can you tell us what we do here?"

If your answer is any combination of the following and incorporates the word *stuff*, you're already losing control of the interview:

> "You build software stuff?"
> "Store stuff?"
> "Let people log in and do stuff?"
> "Stuff?"

Organizations invest significant amounts of time, effort and money in promoting themselves in their online and social media presence. You'd be surprised at the number of organizations that have strong presences on Instagram or Snapchat. You have all the resources in the world to access the life history of the organization you are interviewing for. Use that long bus ride or walk to download and consume as much information as you can before you arrive at the interview.

Take the time to research the organization you are interviewing with, what they stand for, what they want to accomplish and where they are headed. Do it so you can jump through the easy questions and get to the hard questions that will put your drive on display.

Hint: when I have asked this question at an interview and the response is, "I couldn't find time in my schedule to look it up because I was really busy this week," that's code for "I don't want this job."

Follow-up hint: seeing an interviewee check out my LinkedIn profile isn't an ego hit; it shows me how much they want the job.

Just Say No

No, this isn't an antidrug campaign (but if you're wavering, don't do drugs).

If you cannot answer "I don't know" to a question, you've shown me that you are a little cagey. And that makes the little voice in my head question whether, when the chips are down and we're investigating a customer problem, I would be able to count on you to be up-front and able to give me the straight goods on how bad it is.

I've thrown out completely inane questions in interviews, some completely ridiculous, only to see if the candidate would say "I don't know the answer" and not attempt to bluff their way through it.

It's not meant to be mean; it's not meant to make fun of someone or have a good laugh afterward with peers. It's to make sure that when they don't know the answer, they will tell me by saying...

I. Don't. Know.

No one knows everything about everything (that's the point of being part of a team). Your team is going to be counting on you to let them know when you don't know the answer. They need that honesty and vulnerability to help them move forward.

You Are Interviewing with a Company, Not a Person

With all your nervousness and anxiety about being interviewed, it's easy to forget that your interview is not only with the person sitting directly in front of you but also with the company as a whole. I have nothing but the utmost respect for the office managers, administrators and receptionists I have worked with. They do the work that makes our work possible (and removes all barriers from it). At the end of each interview, I always follow up with them about how the candidate acted when they first arrived: Were they polite? Were they demanding? How did they treat the support staff?

This can be a deal breaker. I don't want to hear, "They came in and demanded I hang up their coat, validate their parking and get them a drink, all without a thank-you." You might have wowed us in the formal part of the interview, but you bombed on the informal part.

Forget All That—Watch Me Code

This is probably going to irk some die-hard developers out there, but here goes: I think coding tests are for the birds. They harken back to when you were in university or college and someone put a test in front of you to validate your memory skills and how well you could regurgitate facts.

Go do a search for coding tests and you'll find all the common themes within them.

Translation: they are all following the same patterns.

If you can code Java, you can learn C#. If you can code Node.js, I'm sure you can segue to Python. If you've been working in SQL, I have faith you'll make it to Oracle. Instead, show me what you've done, draw it out on our holiest of tools—our Whiteboard—and impress me with what you've created.

In that instant when the candidate puts marker to board, I know what they have done by how fast they are scribbling out boxes and arrows and talking about what part they wrote, what someone else did, what did and didn't work.

When someone shows up for an interview with a demo of some of the tools that we are currently using to show us what they did over the last few nights before coming in to meet us, that's the candidate we want to hire. Having your demo break in front of us and watching the steps you work through to debug it? That's the drive we're looking for, and that's much more valuable than any written test.

Why Do You Need to Control the Interview?

Tech companies' inboxes are all overflowing with résumés. There are companies geared solely toward filtering content down to the company you are interviewing with. Your grades, your school, your experience—it's all right there next to everyone else's information. Competition is fierce and the interview is your opportunity to set yourself apart from the rest of the pack.

The reason you need to control the interview and wrestle it from the interviewer is because you know something they don't. You know the job you are interviewing for is not the only one you are applying for; *that job* hasn't been posted yet and maybe doesn't even exist. What your interviewer does know (if they are a good interviewer) is that they are going to need someone like you who can make that transition should they need to pivot and make that insane leap.

They aren't only interviewing for today; they're interviewing for tomorrow and for what comes next, and you need to show them that you're the person they need in order for them to be successful.

Can We Focus on the Right Perks?

Perks are cool and fun, but if you're comparing job offers based on perks, I hope you're comparing the right perks.

What projects will you be on?

What platforms will you be using?

What learning opportunities will be available to you?

Who will you be working with on the team?

How will you be pushed and kicked to constantly improve?

What opportunities for growth will you have?

What customers will you be working with?

These are the perks that should be keeping you up at night. A $25,000 espresso machine and hydro massage bar are not perks. They are today's gimmicks and will be replaced by some other gimmick in the next six months.

Make sure you're comparing the right perks.

Stop Worrying about Being the "Best" Coder

There is a fallacy (hopefully debunked by now) that the "best" coders get hired first and will subsequently be promoted first, that every opportunity will come to them first and that they will always have first right of refusal because they are the "best."

No, they won't, simply because there is no such thing as the "best" coder. But for argument's sake, what do you think it takes to be the "best" coder?

> Your ability to work on both front- and back-ends?
> Your extensive database knowledge?
> The speed at which you can get your tasks completed?
> The low level of your bug return count?
> The number of tasks you take on in comparison to other team members?
> The fact that you know red, yellow and blue only work together on a kids' website?
> The ease with which you can decompose the problem?
> Your uncanny ability to show up on time to every meeting and never take sick time?

And this is only a condensed list; there are a thousand other facets that can be considered as we rank ourselves against others in our team.

I'll be the first to admit that I have never been the "best" coder anywhere I've ever worked.

I'm a *good* coder, but I will never be the "best" coder. I'm the guy that Intellisense was built for. I constantly find myself looking up the most rudimentary patterns I have used for years. My memory simply doesn't work that way. But what I do know is how to write code that gets shipped into production and keeps humming. I put effort into ensuring that my code is maintainable, readable and scalable.

I'm not going to expend hours focusing on getting stack exception traces logged across a multitude of log files concurrently in a variety of farms that ship back to a main source. I will put in a significant amount of effort to provide context around what the user was doing when the error occurred so the person reading the log file (i.e., not me but someone from customer support) knows what they need to do next, without having to call me.

Are some of these ranking criteria better than others?
Should we all be measured in the same way?
Is one way really the "best"?

Not a chance. We each have our own "best," and when our "bests" are combined (just got some Captain Planet chills there), we are a pretty powerful, incredible and unstoppable team.

The "best" coder does not exist and never will. You can be a Rock star, Ninja, Wizard, Pilgrim, Explorer, Samurai, Hobbit coder, but you will never be the "best" coder.

What does matter is getting onto a team with a bunch of people who are all good coders with skills that complement your own, raising your game all day, every day.

‹Can You Go the Distance?›

Ask anyone on your team if they want feedback and their first answer will be "Yes, please, I want feedback. I love it, I need it, please keep it coming." Give that same person feedback on their recent efforts and how receptive they actually are to it will depend on how much they "really wanted it."

Herein lies the problem: people want feedback if it's good, but when it's something else, they might not want to hear it. Therefore, it's important for you to know what they are asking for—validation or feedback. Both are okay. But there is a huge difference between them.

If you're driven to constantly, iteratively get better at what you do, you'll want real feedback, not the "You're doing great, so keep doing what you're doing" variety—that's validation and it's only nice to hear when you are seeking out validation, not feedback.

An invested leader will never give you that kind of feedback. They will sit you down and give you the good, the bad and the ugly because they recognize that look in your eyes and they know they can't wiggle out of it.

Remember that goofy little presentation deck I wrote in university? I received the feedback from the class loud and clear—they were not the audience for this type of work. The professor was, and that's who I needed to focus on.

Being driven is about taking that feedback, making hard decisions, pushing through and not faltering or blowing up at someone, keeping your cool and setting yourself up for the long game.

Nothing Takes Two Minutes

Everyone wants their project to be done yesterday, at half the cost and five times the quality, with zero downtime. And everyone needs to get over that. Today.

Developers have to work insanely fast, faster than anyone else on the team, and our drive makes us seem superhuman. We're not. We're just driven.

When you are the new person on the team, there is a pulse of excitement, curiosity and eagerness that courses through your body. You are the sponge and you want more. The day your manager (or perhaps your manager's manager) shows up at your desk asking if you can solve a problem in the next two minutes before the client shows up for the big demo is the day that pulse becomes an injection of adrenaline that will give you goose bumps and have your hair standing on end.

Can you fix this?

Can you save us?

It's hard not to say yes with that much adrenaline and emotion pumping through your veins in that single instant—pride, happiness, inclusion, confidence, appreciation, excitement. You feel like the only answer is yes.

Yes, yes, yes, yes, a million times over. (Why does this sound like the response to a marriage proposal?)

When it should really be no.

No, no, no. (Not the best answer to a marriage proposal.)

When you are saying yes, in that moment, here is how you are thinking things will pan out:

1 Identify bug (well, they already told me where it was)

2 Find offending code (it's in code I know)

3 Fix bug (that's what I'm here for)

4 Check in code (because who doesn't love source control)

5 Trigger build (see step 4: this is a gimme)

6 Deploy build (throw me a parade)

Six quick, easy steps. You control the majority of them, and all of those steps combined (again, Captain Planet) will be done in two minutes.

But it never happens that way. Here's how it eventually turns out:

1 Identify bug (what they thought was the bug wasn't the bug)

2 Try to fix bug (let's give this a shot)

3 Check in code (hail to the king, baby)

4 Trigger build (hoo boy, lots of people are running builds today)

5 Break build (what?)

6 Fix bug again because you forgot to compile before you checked it in (okay, it builds, and if it builds, it runs)

7 Check in code (this time with much shorter comments)

8 Trigger build (hail to the prince, baby—because I threw away my crown on step 4)

9 Deploy build (aha, let's do this)

10 Break some other piece of code, miss an edge case or, worse, fail to fix the bug (well, this is awkward)

11 Finally fix bug (phew, that was tougher than I thought)

12 Check in code (at this point, the comments are taking on a more aggravated tone—Finally, done!)

13 Trigger build (hail to the pauper, baby)

14 Deploy build (All good, man . . . hey, where is everybody?)

This happens all the time. Perhaps it's happening to you right now.

If you don't believe me, go check the comment history from the last time you said it would take you or a colleague two minutes to fix a "quick" bug. The comment history tells it all; you went from six steps to fourteen because you "had" to do it in two minutes.

I have stood by someone's desk and watched as they tried to impress me with how fast they could get it done. I have been that guy as I tried to impress someone standing behind me. It's not easy. The hero complex (more on this later) surges within you as you feel yourself wanting to save the day.

But it never works out that way.

After the first or second miscue of check-ins and failed builds, the person standing at your desk starts to back away slowly, muttering something about it being "no big deal" or saying, "It's okay. Maybe you can put it back the way it was and I'll dance around it."

It's over; you lost.

When you realize work never takes two minutes, the story goes down a different path.

You are up-front that it's going to take ten minutes instead of two for you to code, build, deploy and validate the bug. You can justify your response by showcasing your knowledge of the problem set by asking questions. Instead of taking their instructions as gospel, identify what steps need to be taken. You can up your professionalism quotient by providing a well-thought-out and realistic response.

If you're on fire, you'll bring someone else in to do some surrounding testing while you code this one problem to ensure nothing else is broken.

When I hear from a developer that it will realistically take ten minutes to solve the problem, I am relieved to hear this. In that instant, I know that this developer is considering the problem at hand and at the same time giving me the tools necessary to prepare our client for the changes.

Nothing takes two minutes. Learn it. Embrace it.

You might be wondering right now, *Well, why doesn't my manager simply buffer all my estimates or assume it will take that much longer based on my track record?*

Is that what you want your manager to be doing? Buffering everything you do? What happens when you switch jobs? Do you inform your new manager of the buffer protocol that must be implemented for you to be successful?

Doubtful. You need to remember that the goal is not for someone else to get better at estimating your work, it's for you to get better at estimating it.

Software estimation is a tough topic, one that everyone has an opinion on (including me). We'll get to it later and discuss it from a few different angles.

It's Not a Bug until a Customer Reports It

At my first job, a senior developer told me this when we found a bug in an application we were working on. The translation: we don't start working on problems until they are reported as problems.

Their reasoning? Working on unreported bugs will not boost your metrics and your team leads might not appreciate all the time you put into fixing those issues and stopping them from seeing the light of day. Your team might even question why you are bothering with them since they haven't been found.

Here's why you shouldn't take this approach:

Testers will appreciate your dedication to reducing their workload.

Customers will appreciate your commitment to making their software run smoothly.

And those that come after you who see what you are doing?

Well, now you've started a movement that everyone wants to be a part of.

Embrace Your Grunt Work

In every job, there are tasks that need to get done. They are not the most challenging, gratifying or interesting to work on, but they need to be delivered. This is the grunt work and it is different for everyone. It could be fixing bugs, estimating tasks, doing a code review, updating CSS templates, building unit tests and so on.

Everyone has their own special mix of grunt work. It is part of our job and it is not going anywhere.

I rotated this information between the Drive and Delivery chapters of the book a number of times and finally settled on putting it in Drive because even though grunt work needs to be delivered, it's our drive that makes it happen.

I have always struggled with writing unit tests because I find them boring and unimaginative. I recognize the need but don't always have the drive to push myself to not only complete them but also keep them up-to-date.

Instead of writing standard unit tests, I found solace in writing little console or web applications that would execute my code in the same way but let me work on some other skills at the same time. I eventually came to accept that my sweet little test apps were no longer a benefit to the team and only served one purpose—to make me feel better. Now I do my grunt work, build my unit tests, connect them to the builds, watch them pass or fail, and adjust them from there.

The hidden truth behind embracing our grunt work is that it is the gateway to some of our greatest software inventions. Entire organizations have been founded on grunt-work tasks—i.e., unit tests, code reviews, refactoring, logging, form creation, authentication. (Seriously, someone started a company to make refactoring easier... Refactoring!)

Where did all these ideas come from?

From driven people like you, doing the grunt work and figuring out how to make it better, reduce the time involved, automate the process and kick it to the curb. We are never too important, never too good, for grunt work. It's the work that has the potential to provide you with the most profound ideas to make something better.

Release the Kraken

The kraken is a mythical beast that could only be unleashed by Hades... now and again. When unleashed, the kraken was destruction incarnate. Nothing could stop it as it raged against everything, leaving death and destruction in its wake.

If the kraken was released every day, would it have the same energy?

Probably not. Leaving a wake of destruction in your path takes a lot out of you.

And that's the point. You might be able to go full tilt sixteen hours a day, not stopping for a full week as you push toward that final GA build, but eventually you are going to crash and you are going to crash hard.

You gave it your all to get that release across the finish line, but now that it's there, it's time to pull it back and take a breather. Our drive is at our peak when the kraken is released, but we can't maintain that drive forever. Take a breather, get some rest and remember that releasing the kraken is good, but not every day.

Go Faster by Going Slower

Krakens are great, but, as I said, releasing the kraken every day can have disastrous consequences.

Have you ever gone for a drive through the mountains? I'm not talking nice, smooth, grassy, rolling hills. I'm talking *mountains*. As you are driving up, you peer down at the drop, thinking about all the mistakes you've made in life and whether today is karma's shining moment.

As you push to the top as fast as you can, you think the hardest part will be getting to the peak of the moutain and then you'll get to enjoy the relaxing ride down the back.

But the cruise down isn't quite what you thought. Gravity is pushing you down those long stretches, and eventually you find yourself having to brake hard on the winding turns that you don't see coming, or you'll jump the barrier. All the while, this ferocious starting and stopping is slowly hurting you. Your engine is burning out as you put more and more pressure on it until your tires start to smoke with an acrid smell of burnt rubber.

The kraken has hit a wall.

When you are driving down a mountain, the solution is to drop a gear and adopt a more steady, consistent speed that will prevent you from having to stop and start when an obstacle pops out in front of you. That way, you don't arrive battered, bruised and in need of major repairs (because this happens in real life).

The pressure is always on in software development to deliver yesterday.

Identifying when you need to drop a gear starts with you.

You need to be the voice of reason and sanity when everyone's losing their head to get the problem resolved. You need to show them the path to delivery without taking on more technical debt, without omitting critical test cases and without impacting the customer.

The interweb is littered with fixes that went out too fast and cost companies more than the fix was worth... all because we needed it done yesterday.

Dropping a gear isn't going to slow down your drive; it's going to ensure you have something left in the tank when you need it.

You Won't Win a Trophy for Burning Out

You get the picture, I'm sure. If you're constantly hammering yourself to release the kraken and never entering that steady state, you're on your way to burning out.

Perhaps you've convinced yourself that when you're in this loop, you are "in the zone" and making it work, but really you are one hot feature away from going over the edge.

It'll hit you on a small thing that you would not normally bat an eye over. You react in a way that's out of character, and when you walk away, you instantly realize what a complete jerk you were.

The key to avoiding burnout is knowing your triggers and how to avoid them.

It took me a few years to figure out mine, but now I know when burnout is starting to happen and when implosion is imminent. Oddly enough, it doesn't start with random explosions of emotions; instead I become very quiet, very focused on the path I'm on, and I have little desire to switch it up, deviate or interact with anyone. I become very inflexible, conversation and niceties go out the window, and my dry wit turns into sharp, biting sarcasm.

And I regret it. I immediately regret it. I regret it years after it happens.

We all do.

Everybody wants to be the hero, but you're no good if you're a crispy piece of bacon with nothing left to give (and burnt, black bacon is the saddest kind of bacon because it had the potential to be so much more). If you're reading this and it's resonating with where you are right now in your current job, put down the book, go outside, and think about where you are and what you are doing.

The best way to get out of burnout is to talk to someone—your manager, your project lead, a colleague, anyone. It doesn't have to follow that order, but if the first person you talk to doesn't acknowledge you and offer to help, keep moving on until you find someone who will, whether they are in your immediate organization or not. Take a moment, get their feedback and adjust.

Being driven does *not* mean burning out.

What about Your Feedback?

If you want to grow, you need feedback.

Not pat-on-the-back feedback, but real feedback that points out where you're struggling, reestablishes your focus and gives you a renewed sense of energy and confidence.

This is about you getting that feedback, fighting for it and demanding it. (How to give it comes later.)

Driven developers ask for feedback when none is being given.

It can be informal: "Hey, can you take a look at this?"

Or it can be formal: "Hey, can we sit down and discuss how I'm doing?"

Informal feedback is off-the-cuff and delivered at your desk or on the way out to get a burger for lunch.

Formal feedback is a sit-down (perhaps over that burger) after the person whom you are asking for feedback has had time to prepare, so they can think about how things are going and make suggestions.

The only caveat to getting feedback is that once you put out the request for it, it's on you to receive it. To take the good, the bad and the ugly, and to figure out your next steps.

Those who are driven only want the bad and the ugly; they couldn't care less about the good because they know what they are good at. If you find yourself arguing about the feedback you've received, it could be because you're not listening and you're not ready to hear it.

I have found that people on the verge of burnout always want feedback just as they are about to burn out. They need some validation or a hit of dopamine to keep themselves going—it's their fuel. In these cases, I won't bite. I'll wait for the project to be over and things to settle, because whatever I say is not going to be what they want to hear.

Feedback does not need to come from your immediate manager; it can come from other managers or people in your organization whom you engage with. If you find that the feedback coming from your immediate manager is not helping you to grow and it's more of the same "atta boy/girl, keep it up," then seek out someone else who will give you the lowdown you're looking for.

Drivers seek out feedback in all its forms and eschew validation.

‹Will You Stand Out?›

Standing out isn't about being the most confident, well-spoken, charismatic, eager-to-please developer on the team.

It's about becoming the member of your team who gets it done.

How fast can you become a contributing member to your team?

How will you begin sowing the seeds of leadership that will make people start to gravitate toward you because they want to work with and beside you, learning from you in order to follow in your footsteps?

How will you set yourself apart from everyone else?

Fail till you can't fail anymore and then fail again.

I'm a big fan of trying out new ideas and concepts and messing them up.

This is probably one of the reasons I don't find myself compelled to adopt any particular methodology of software development. Instead, I seek to take the best of all of them and see what fits the situation at hand.

Want to try out a new design pattern? Go for it.

Want to go Agile? Sure, why not.

Liking that Waterfall? Sounds good.

Want to try a new library? Download it.

Not sure what that keyword does? Use it.

As long as you are not deploying broken builds to a customer site, developing inconsistent user interfaces or delivering otherwise buggy features into your code, you should be encouraged to experiment and try new approaches. It is only through the understanding of different approaches that we start to bring new ideas to the table and expand our knowledge across a wide variety of platforms—taking the best of all worlds to create incredible software.

By trade, I focus pretty much entirely on the .NET stack, but I didn't start there. I have dabbled pretty heavily in PHP/MySQL and a number of other languages over the years.

Learning different constructs and approaches in a new language often leads to ideas to solving problems in another (and it's fun to transport concepts from one into the other).

You're young, you're coding all the time, so go out, have some fun and experiment a bit. (We are talking solely about code here.)

Build things, break things, start over again.

Code is meant to be built, then broken, then built again, then broken again.

And pay it forward. Encourage those you work with to keep on breaking things and to never stop experimenting.

We have source control—branch it, code it, demo it and do it again.

Are You Ready to Sit at the Table?

Remember what you were being interviewed for? The job that didn't exist? Well, here it is. This is where you take the wheel.

If you're now being offered a team lead or manager role, the following will be a continual loop running through your mind at a frenetic pace:

> Where do I start?
> What's the first step?
> What comes next?
> How do I help people when they come to me with a problem I don't understand?
> How do I handle someone's failure when they're trying something new?
> How do I keep my own skills up-to-date in case this doesn't work out?
> Am I ready for this?

> Do I tell people what to do now?
> Will they listen to me?
> Will they want to listen to me?
> Should we be eating lunch together?

And this is the short list.

But here are the two questions you need to be asking yourself:

> Am I ready to sit at the table?
> Am I ready to make the hard decisions that I've always thought about?

Most people immediately say, "Yes, give me the extra responsibility. I'm ready." But most aren't.

Being a great leader for your team involves a certain level of self-awareness. You'll be constantly evaluating yourself—how you are doing, what you are working on, where you need to improve, what works, what doesn't. Rinse and repeat.

In the Leadership chapter of the book, we'll dig much deeper into this role, but the key point I want to make here is that there is nothing wrong with turning down a leadership role when it's first offered to you. There will be no backlash if you say no; you are still as driven as ever if you say no. In the event that you do say no, one of two things will happen. One, the company will ask what they can do to help you get ready (because they believe in you and they know who they hired). Or two, they will never offer you anything again.

You want to stay with the company that offers help. The company that doesn't is a mistake you've made, and it's probably a good thing you rejected the role if this is their response to your authenticity and honesty.

I turned down leadership roles twice because I knew I wasn't ready for what was going to come at me. I didn't have what I perceived as the correct level of coding experience, and I wasn't ready to start leading people, knowing all that was required to be successful at it.

Before jumping in, ask yourself if you are ready.

Forget about What People Think

As a new leader, this is the first rule that you need to start repeating to yourself on a daily—and, if needed, hourly—basis.

After receiving a promotion, many new leaders worry way too much about how they are perceived by their team, their leaders and other groups. Our perception about these thoughts are in overdrive as we try to be everything to everyone and let other people's responses guide our actions.

It starts off simply:

> ➤ *I'm not as strong as X...*
> ➤ *I should have realized this sooner...*
> ➤ *I took too long on that last fix...*

It doesn't matter how many more excuses you came up with internally; all that matters is that you forget what they are thinking and focus on you and your team. Not everyone is willing to do what you are doing; complaining is easy for those who think they can do better but never end up doing anything.

Lead like You Develop

When you were a new developer, you took risks all the time to see what did and didn't work so that you could help your product, project and team be better. You stuck with what worked and ditched what didn't, but you always kept trying new approaches.

You weren't promoted into this position to maintain the status quo, to not rock the boat and to not change anything.

As long as you are always acting with your team's best interests and outcome in mind, give your ideas a shot, figure out what works and what doesn't, and forget what everyone else thinks.

You are going to screw things up, you are going to make mistakes, you are going to wish you had gone with your gut on some decisions, but by being honest and building trust with your people, you will keep getting better and better at leading.

When your team sees you doing all those things—whether you succeed or fail—they will see the level of effort you have put in. They won't criticize it; they'll be emboldened by it and will look to do the same.

Forget the optics; light the fires and get driving.

Find Your Cave

Have you ever heard the expression "I'm going into a cave to work on X"—whatever X is? I've heard it a number of times, and I've even used it myself. The cave is where you do your best work, where no one can find you, where you can't reach anyone, where the only thing before you is the problem to solve. The cave can be your local coffee shop with all the commotion happening around you, the library, the storage closet in the basement, your kids' playroom after they have gone to sleep, the office hallway that no one goes down. It can be whatever you want.

But it's your cave, it's your place, it's where your best work comes from and where you rise to the challenge day in and day out. The cave isn't where you hide from the big problems of the day. You don't go there when there are fires all around you and people need you; this isn't about hiding in a cave and waiting for the storm to blow over.

This is about finding the place where you operate beyond peak efficiency, where you can unleash everything you do to be a success.

Find that spot and go there when you need to get work done, but don't hide there.

Consistency Is the Key to Coding Leadership

Consistency as a leader is paramount to your success. Your team is going to be looking to you for guidance, and if they see you acting like a kid in a candy store, getting distracted by shiny wrappers and gumball machines, then they will do the same.

Managers are great at documenting change, creating the PowerPoint deck, reviewing it and making sure everyone on the team knows what the change is and what is expected of them.

Leaders implement the change they want to see in themselves first and iron out the kinks along the way. The only PowerPoint decks they are putting together are the ones that say, "This is what we did and how we did it."

Be consistent in your approach to new ideas and always lead them.

You Are the Linchpin

I saved this for the end.

Everyone has a part to play in the delivery of software: product managers, testers, customer support, technical writers, trial managers, and the list goes on. At the end of it all, you, the developer, invariably become the linchpin of it all. This isn't an ego trip and you shouldn't take it as one. (*Do not take it as one.*) Take a look at everything you are being asked to do: disseminate requirements, create designs, build code, deploy code, deliver code, fix bugs in code, troubleshoot topologies, write deployment plans, assist with problems on trial sites, work with customer support to enabling logging, work with the customer, etc., etc.

At the end of the day, it all comes back to you, the linchpin.

Aside from encouraging your head to grow to epic proportions, what value does this message serve?

It's a reminder to be humble.

The secret is out, and now it's time for you to humbly accept that mantle of responsibility and all that comes with it.

When you are the linchpin, you are the educator for many, you are the day-long question-answerer, you are the reviewer of documentation, you are the helper of trial sites, you are the idea person behind that new library that will save your team hours upon hours of work, and you are still the writer of unbreakable code.

You are the driver.

Remain humble, respect those around you, and realize that without your team, you are not going to get anywhere on this project.

You might be at the epicenter of it all, but you are not *the* epicenter of it all.

Humility is the origin of your leadership story.

You can easily go the other way and let everyone know that you are the linchpin on this and every other project that you have led before. Let them know that you are indispensable; remind them of it each and every day so they never forget. You could do that, and you would fail.

The linchpins who humble themselves are the ones who are surrounded by peers and colleagues when something goes wrong with their code or they need help to finish their work.

The linchpins stand up in a meeting and suggest a new course of action, without shutting down the previous action, while at the same time inspiring the rest of the team to jump on board to help out.

The linchpins volunteer to come in on the weekend and help with testing and documentation efforts, recognizing the importance of every task in the overall delivery effort and knowing that one person alone cannot do it.

And linchpins do it all while making everyone else on their team, and in the company, feel as though they are the linchpins too.

Linchpins stand out, but they make sure that they are not seen as standouts.

‹TL;DR›

We've all worked with team members who blew us away with their commitment, their dedication, their zeal, their excitement, their sense of purpose, their passion—they are all drive, focused drive.

They aren't afraid to ask themselves the tough questions, be aware of what they are doing and find the path that works for them.

Great drivers don't wait for someone to say, "Okay, now you can start" or "Should we do this?" They have their own plan in mind, they take control of the situation from the start and they execute on it. They will stumble. They have to in order to find out what works, but they are committed to going the distance and they realize that the game is long.

This chapter might have felt like a ton of bricks coming down on you all at once. Maybe you even feel a bit overwhelmed by everything you've read and are wondering if that can be you. *Am I that person?*

You might be thinking, *Do I have to go out and announce that I am all these things now?* Certainly not. The best developers I have worked with, people whose drive eclipsed my own, had completely different personalities than mine. They found out which components of drive made them a success, they asked themselves the hard questions and they got started.

That's what's up to you—how driven are you?

3

INITIATIVE

nitiative is leading the Army of One. If you are going to lead and inspire others to do the same, you will need to lead yourself first. You will need to demonstrate how to set and achieve your own goals. This isn't about following the herd and doing what everyone else is doing; this is about carving your own path.

How many times have you heard the following from colleagues?

"I don't want to lead. If I start leading, I'll have to stop coding, and then I'll become obsolete."

Really? You can't do both? Who said so?

"I'm not good enough to work on that project because I don't understand NoSQL."

Really? Someone deleted the internet and you can't find anything related to NoSQL to teach yourself?

"I know we need more people for this project, but you can't give me any more."

Great, no outside hires, so how about internal ones? Who wants to jump in and join in the fun?

Initiative is the kick you give yourself all day, every day, to get "it" done (whatever "it" is).

Drive sets you up to get there, but the next step is all initiative, and sadly, this is where we lose people. Initiative is fraught with many unknowns. You'll be pushed out of your comfort zone and often feel like you don't measure up.

If you're feeling this way right now, good. It means you're breaking through; it means you're starting to ask the right questions, and if you stop now, you're going to miss out.

Without initiative, we are superstars, rock stars and ninjas but only in our heads.

When we think about initiative, there are three questions which guide us:

1 Why are you holding back?
2 Who is running the show?
3 Are you the Army of One?

‹Why Are You Holding Back?›

Not *who* is holding you back, not *what* is holding you back, but *why* are you holding back. This is the question that defines initiative because it forces us to put down the keyboard and think long and hard about why we are holding ourselves back.

What is stopping me from achieving my goals?

Why am I doing all the work but getting passed over again and again?

Why am I letting "others" hold me back?

What am I waiting for?

All of these questions (and likely more) are rooted in why you are holding yourself back.

Craptivity

I'm leading with this because this is the source of our internal questioning, bickering, frustration, confusion and every other emotion that causes us to start something and then give up.

When an artist creates art for the first time, they struggle with getting what is in their head—what is perfect, beautiful, pristine and of such amazing quality—onto the canvas.

If you were to start drawing today (or doing any other activity you've never done before), you'd probably look at your drawing and exclaim, "That is incredible. I put pen to paper and drew a stick man. It's all onwards and upwards from here." It's the same feeling you have when you go to the gym for the first time in months, finish one workout, look at yourself in the mirror and think, *Yes, this is going great.*

But as the artist grows and starts to develop their own style, that initial euphoria begins to wear off. They struggle to replicate those same feelings while trying to grow. Their work isn't as new and fresh as it used to be. As they focus on new patterns and techniques, the art comes off as forced and awkward, invariably showing signs of the internal struggle and frustration as the artist tries to leap to the next level. The artist looks back in awe at what they did at the beginning and wonders how they could have fallen so far from where they first started.

Truth is, they've gotten better, but right now they are mired in the toughest stage of learning—craptivity.

Craptivity is the stage where you are on the precipice of getting better at your craft, but you can't see it. It's the infinite battle between where you are and where you want to be, and there's no clear direction in front of you for how to get there. In developer terms, it's the stage where people comment on your abilities as "knowing enough to be dangerous."

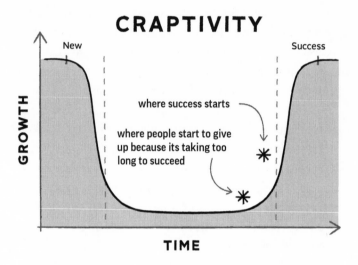

You're building "goodish" stuff but not the great masterpieces you aspire to. To make matters worse, you see others building masterpieces, and it feels as though you are hitting wall after wall and you can't turn the corner.

Threading, concurrency, performance, debugging, provisioning, authentication, automation and scale are all concepts that you might have struggled with at one point in time but have now powered through (or perhaps you're still fighting them). They are the complex topics that we need to learn and understand in order to reach that gold standard of code and be successful.

Craptivity now becomes our enemy. It holds on, pushing us down, wanting us to give up and try something new (because something new must be easier) rather than pushing forward and seeing this monolithic thing to completion.

This stage of craptivity is what separates the good from the great developers. The good developers stop where they are and go learn something else, become "jacks of a few trades," while the great developers figure out how to break out of craptivity in order to move on to becoming incredible at all of it.

There is no magic process to get out of craptivity. There is no time frame. There is only you, putting in the effort each and every day to get past it, break free of its hold and realize that no one else is holding you back—not your team lead, not your manager, not the other person who was hired at the same time.

Just you.

Get Yourself a Mantra

If you don't have one, get one.

A sentence fragment, a poem, a YouTube video, a song, a cat poster—find something that gets you motivated, brings you back to life, renews your focus and gives you that swift kick in the butt you need to get out there, get back in your chair and get things done once again.

Initiative is about getting back in the game, pushing forward, not giving up. A mantra—your mantra—is your single best weapon to get there. Find your own; don't share it with anyone. If you are going a step further and creating one for the team (i.e., the traditional sales gong), share that one, but don't ever share yours—it's there for you and you alone.

You don't need a crowd cheering you on or cheerleaders spelling out your name. What you need is your own mantra.

"Go Deep, Take Everything"

When you're all over the place, jumping from opportunity to opportunity, project to project, role to role, over the span of weeks, you have no focus. You're not sure what to do, so you keep trying everything. This might be unavoidable given the fires and incoming priorities coming at you. And this is where you'll blame someone else for "holding you back" from success, because it's their fault.

To be successful, you must have focus, and you must have the kind of focus where people will talk about your persistence, dedication and commitment to getting things done even after you have left. It all starts with you sitting in a room, deciding what that focus will be and where your energy will be spent.

There is a great quote from the old TV show *Heroes*, where the man in horn-rimmed glasses is about to get his memory wiped by the Haitian. He looks up at him and says, "Go deep, take everything." You need to do the same thing in everything you do—go deep, learn everything.

Be Part of What Matters

Everyone wants to work on the uber-awesome projects with the coolest frameworks because why not? That's where all the action and excitement is, and that is what will fuel your growth and development.

The truth is, you won't always be assigned this work, whether it's because the work will be shared across the team, everyone needs a chance, someone else is in line... yada, yada, pick the reason that works for you.

Which is why you shouldn't wait to be asked. Volunteer for the awesome work. Get your name on the list, and if you can't do that, start coding it after-hours so people can see what you can contribute when you're not asked to do it.

Who's going to stop you from doing extra learning?

There will always be grunt work. The best way to eliminate grunt work is to make it worthwhile. Take that new framework and apply it to those lame tasks you have on your bug pile.

If you are working on a project where no one cares when it gets done because it "doesn't matter," make it matter. Figure out how to get eyeballs on it, turn it into something better, bring it to the front page of the discussion, automate it, script it, and/or get rid of it altogether.

Always be working on work what matters, and don't wait for it to be assigned to you to start on it.

The Illusion of Multitasking

No one can multitask in software. Not you, not me, not everyone, not anyone. We are not programmed to execute multi-threaded operations.

I cannot simultaneously check the scores of a baseball game, attend a meeting and give a performance review while applying the same levels of dedication and attention I would if doing each task on its own.

And yet we are always asked to "multitask" as though this is a revolutionary idea.

What we can do is provide the illusion of multitasking, and through that illusion, we can isolate what factors might be contributing to holding us back.

Grab a notepad and think back to your accomplishments from last week. List each day of the week and everything you accomplished on that day—everything.

Take a moment and bask in the glow of your accomplishments.

When finished, take a different-colored pen, marker or highlighter, and note which of these items were known when the week started.

You might end up having a list like this:

MONDAY

- Fixed bugs
- Built new features
- Assisted team with customer issues

TUESDAY

- Reviewed requirements
- Attended some scrums & meetings
- Maintained daily awesomeness
- Had meetings with team

THURSDAY

- Got pulled into design session
- Had customer support ticket escalated to me
- Helped newbie with builds

Were all of these activities planned? Could you have anticipated any of them?

The act of multitasking isn't about doing multiple things concurrently; it's about organizing your work into a pattern where you can accomplish your work in a serial fashion but make it look like it was executed in a parallel fashion.

Hence the illusion.

When approached from this angle, the meaning of multitasking shifts from trying to do things simultaneously to preparation, anticipation and your response to unknown external factors as they come your way.

Go back to your original list, and mark each item with a H, N or W.

What did you *have* to accomplish? (These are the must-dos even if the world was going up in flames.)

What did you *need* to accomplish? (These tasks are important, but they're not critical.)

What did you *want* to accomplish? (These tasks fulfill you and make you feel successful.)

Again, how many of those tasks were planned versus unplanned?

Before your next week starts, make a similar list of everything on your plate and everything that you think is going to come at you during the week.

As the week progresses, some items will move to different categories and you'll push out others, but you should be able to get most of them done.

How?

How did this happen, when all you did was write down a list?

When we know what we *have* to do, *need* to do and *want* to do, the priorities take care of themselves. When new work comes in during the week, we automatically classify it based on this simple system. We indicate which bucket that work should go in, and we do it in plain English that dictates the inherent priority of what needs to get done first.

From here, we parlay this information into discussions with our team: What do we have to do this week? What is needed on this release?

People won't be coming up to you to say, "How did you get all this work done concurrently? Please share with me your secrets for success!"

But they might say, "How did you get all this work done this week?"

That's what you want, and to get started, all you need is paper and pen. No fancy app, no complicated sign-up process—a piece of paper and a pen will suffice.

Build from there.

What's Your Bonus?

There are many factors that we believe are holding us back from achieving our goals and many more stories that we can tell ourselves about why we are not succeeding.

The simple questions generally have the easiest answers. Ask yourself, "What's my bonus?"

What are you going to get from achieving this goal?

What will make you dig in and see it to the end?

Is it your actual end-of-year bonus that pushes you to grow?

Is it being able to pay off your car?

Is it the opportunity to take on new projects and challenges?

Is it sharing the information you learned with others?

Whatever your bonus is, it's yours for the taking. No one else is going to go for it but you. You don't need to broadcast it all over Instagram; you simply need to start working toward it. If you feel like you're the one who's been holding you back, that's good.

If you're thinking, *My bonus is getting this product out the door because I've been working on it for a year*, that's most likely not the case. It's a step toward your true bonus. Getting the first, tenth, hundredth customer to buy your code or having an esteemed member of the community tweet about how great it is—that's the bonus you're after.

‹Who Is Running the Show?›

It's you. It's always been you. You simply forgot and let someone else take the wheel for a while.

That's okay. Now it's time to take it back.

Precious Time

Your time is your currency, and you are the bank. Everyone around you wants to make daily withdrawals, but the only one making deposits is you.

Other people will try to substitute their priorities for yours. Don't let them.

This doesn't mean you start saying, "I don't have time for this. This is your problem, not mine." It does mean you need to figure out what load you can bear to ensure you can get your work done while still helping others.

This isn't about going full Gollum and saying "My Preciousssssss" (*Lord of the Rings* FTW) when someone asks you for help, hoarding your own time for only your goals and no one else's. This strategy might help you today in achieving those goals, but you'll lose the bigger game of achieving your goals while helping people achieve theirs.

The purpose is to understand and invest time in your goals—don't be everything to everyone and don't give up on your goals for everyone else's.

Do Something That No One Will Notice

Initiative is about taking the leap and doing something different. It's about operating on the fringe where everyone else is too scared to go because what you are proposing hasn't been proven, it has too many risks associated with it and no one knows if it will work.

This is the sweet spot and you want to be here.

We will only get there by having one person—you—take the initiative.

If you *are* going to take this leap, here's some advice:

> Don't broadcast it on LinkedIn, Instagram, Facebook, your company intranet, whatever.

> Don't provide status updates on it in a team meeting.

> Don't work it into your next performance review or finagle it into some kind of bonus stretch-goal structure.

Don't tell your team or your managers what you did until they ask, "Hey, when did you do that? I thought we couldn't do that. Everyone said it wouldn't work." Smile, nod and then start on the next thing that can't be done.

Are You Worth $3 a Day?

There are 365 days in a year. If you set aside $3 a day for a year, you would have close to $1,095 to invest in yourself by the end.

What could you do with that $1,095 if you had it all in front of you today?

Invest in a training course subscription?

Purchase a developer cloud subscription to Azure, Google or AWS, and learn some new tricks?

Upgrade your LinkedIn membership to a premium level?

Purchase some IoT hardware to tinker with?

Build your own arcade machine?

Too often we see the sticker price of $15 per month or $500 per year and become a slave to that number. We focus on the output to be charged now versus the return on investment to be yielded 365 days from now.

Initiative is what sets you up for the long game, as you recognize the investment you need to put in today to become a success tomorrow. If you were to invest that $1,095 in yourself today and it secured you a new job with a $5,000 raise, that's just shy of a 400-percent return on your investment.

With your investment comes time and an improvement in what you have to offer.

If you don't have the time to grind for new customers on LinkedIn, work on that new hardware set or watch those online courses, invest your money elsewhere.

How many courses did you watch on your Pluralsight subscription this past year? How long did it take for you to start and finish those Udemy courses you purchased?

In any investment, you need to identify your break-even, the point at which you have recouped your costs and are now into happy-happy profitability territory.

Does taking two courses a month make your investment worthwhile?

Growing your network by twenty-five connections a month?

Being able to port customers to that new platform in six months?

It all comes back to whether you are willing to invest $3 a day in yourself or in that designer coffee with imported pumpkin spice.

What If You Don't Control the Training Dollars?

Doesn't matter.

The same mind-set applies when you're trying to convince your employer that you need (not want) to go to a conference. In that instant, when you are standing at their desk asking for their funds, they are visualizing what it will mean to lose you for that time, their current deliverables and the investment that's required.

It's not a bad thing. They have a business to run. Yes, they will be happy to hear about your initiative to grow, but they need to weigh this against the needs of everyone else on their team and potentially the rest of the company at large.

When this happens, it's the same exercise: meals, travel, conference—let's say $7,500 cost in total. Spread out over a year, that's only $21 per day.

Ask your employer if you are worth that.

They still might say no, but now you've put that number in their head. It might not be until your next one-on-one, when they are heaping praise on you for all that you have done, that you'll ask them if you are worth $21. They might come back to you and say, "Look, I can't do $21 this year. I can do $10. What can I get for $10?"

At $10 a day, you have $3,650 to put together a plan to get better—what will you do?

Attending Conferences versus Building Your Own Training Program

When I was first starting out, whenever I switched jobs or roles, people were always on me to check what the external, formal training opportunities were before I signed on. Translation: what conferences would they offer to send me on? Everyone loves a good conference—the team bonding, the meals, the drinks, the fire hose of knowledge coming at you from over seventy in-depth sessions, over forty breakouts and umpteen working sessions with colleagues from around the world. It's an experience that we all look forward to (for some, it happens every year). While learning new trends and technology in our industry is great, it's not the best form of training for you to be undertaking year after year.

Conferences are safe, they are clean, they have snacks and they are predictable in how they unfold; you know what is happening every second of every day. It's a walk around the convention floor, a game to grab as much swag as you can, and then you sit back, relax and listen to what is being said.

It's the training you think you want, but it's not the training you need.

The best training for you right now is the informal training you can receive while working on the job. The training that you didn't know was "training" at the time, but now, when you look back on it, you instantly know it was the best training you ever received.

I'm talking about these experiences:

> The late nights you spend debugging issues with a coworker because some random scenario has reared its ugly head and you need to figure out what is what.

> That last-minute customer call where the customer is losing their mind over the latest upgrade and you've been brought in with your team lead to try to defuse the situation.

> The sales presentation you're pulled into, where the prospective customer has some technical questions on the implementation that only you can answer, but you need to answer them in a way that inspires confidence so the customer will buy your product.

> The hectic few days when you have to learn a new SDK so you can integrate it into a feature for the QA deployment next week.

This is the training that will make you grow by leaps and bounds.

There is no "informal training" session that you are going to be able to sign up for months in advance. These are events that will happen at the last minute, when people will be looking around the room for someone to step up and make it happen. Take every opportunity you can to make yourself a part of these situations to learn and grow.

If you are going to attend a conference and you know you will be the person on the Slack channel working on problems back at the office and thereby missing out on what's being said, *don't go*. You're not committed, it's not for you, give someone else the opportunity to live and breathe it.

Watch the keynote online, download the courses when they are released after the conference, read up on it later, but don't actually go.

Don't go solely to say you had a drink from the fire hose. Instead, build your own training program for $3 a day.

You'll get more out of it.

Overtake Them on the Hill

Many years ago (too many, in fact), I undertook the task of running a half marathon (twenty-one kilometers in Canada) and trained for it in seven weeks. I had a friend who was an accomplished marathoner helping me with my training regimen.

The best piece of advice she gave me was, "Overtake them on the hill."

When these words of wisdom were first imparted to me, I didn't understand them and my initial response was, "Look, I'm trying to finish this thing. Whatever happens, happens."

But when the race started, I observed people slowing down as they reached the base of the hills. They changed their stance, shook out their arms a little more, and took a few moments to catch their breath as they approached the hill.

They were slowing down because an obstacle was coming up in front of them. They were anticipating the obstacle and slowing down in advance because of the change it represented. They knew that when you run up a hill, your body uses a different set of muscles and your legs compensate for not only the change in incline but also the change in posture, and as a result, your speed changes.

In that brief moment, you have two options: slow down and follow the others *or* overtake them and lead. When you overtake, you are setting the new pace and you are setting the expectations; you are working while others are resting.

Initiative is about leading the Army of One, and, like running, it's about pushing yourself to get there.

‹Can You Lead the Army of One?›

How do you get there? How do you get to achieving your goals and ambitions, becoming unstuck, leaping over others in front of you, succeeding where others fail?

You make the decision to lead yourself or no one at all.

Own Your Goals

This isn't a how-to on the proper rules and disciplines for setting your own goals and all the methodologies you need to apply to make it happen. There is enough literature out there on this topic that I would not do any of it justice.

We all struggle with goal setting, and we all have our own approaches, but oftentimes it's the simplest idea that works. The only guidance I will offer on goals is to keep them manageable. Take that big mammoth thing you want to do (be a better developer, let's say) and spend ten minutes focusing on what that means (i.e., learning new frameworks, learning "the cloud," understanding user experience design), break it down into manageable learning chunks and schedule it into your daily life.

Now start chipping away at that mountain and don't worry about the end result (the goal). Just chip.

That's it, that's all I have. Take the big, and make it small. Chip away at the pile. Don't ever look at what is left on the pile, but constantly work toward reducing it. If your goals are like mine, that pile will never get smaller, but the "what I've accomplished pile" that sits right beside it will get bigger, and that's where you'll win.

I did a Spartan Race a number of years ago with absolutely zero training. (I have no idea why.)

The event was held on a ski run where you had to run up five ski hills as part of the course. It was a grueling course, and the heat was blistering. Already exhausted and dehydrated, I turned what I thought was the last corner and instead stood at the base of another hill. In that instant, a crushing wave of despair, frustration and anger rolled through me. It was one of those few times when I stood for a good five minutes thinking, *Nope, not doing this.* (There were many other words, but you get the gist.) Today, there would be no overtaking them on the hill, and all I wanted to do in that moment was walk away.

As I stood there, a woman (clearly someone who had put way more planning into this event and was in way better shape than I) was consoling one of her friends who was feeling the same way I was, so I stood there and listened to one of the most amazing pep talks I've ever heard:

> "Don't look up. Look at your feet, put one foot in front of the other and focus on doing that and only that. You will make it to the top, you will get there, you will conquer this mountain and finish—but only if you focus on your feet."

At the time, my initial response was "duh." (Cue more profanity.) But it was enough for me to start (and that's the key). As I trudged up that hill, I could feel people running past me, but I never looked up at them or anything else. There could have been a forest fire around me and I would not have looked up.

My eyes were glued to my feet, one going in front of the other in an almost hypnotic pattern. Eventually I made it to the top and almost collapsed when I saw how far I had come. (It could have been dehydration, but I'm going to go with elation.)

My advice is to find the pattern that works for you, keep it manageable and focus on what you are doing each and every day to chip away at that goal. One day it will be done. Remember *have-need-want*.

They are your goals and no one else's. As long as the accomplished pile is greater than your to-do pile, you're on the right track.

Step Up

Simply put, volunteering for projects, committees, events and customer visits will enable you to demonstrate that you are able to not only take on more but do it well. Volunteering is a great way to try something new with little or no downside. It doesn't need to be volunteering outside of your company either; you can do it internally. Once we start getting paid for our work, we forget about what our real paycheck is and every now and again we need a reminder about what matters most.

Build a Community

This is a tough one because it involves putting yourself out there. I struggle with the entire social media thing from A to Z, but I wholeheartedly believe that the best way to start getting your thoughts out into the open so people can see all that you can do is to start a blog. Don't worry about the audience and who's reading it. Just start writing about what you know and what you are working on.

If you have a different approach to solving a problem, keep it generic and write about it.

If you recently wrote a cool extension to a library, write about it and share on github.

Don't worry about who sees it or how many likes or followers you get. Do put it on your LinkedIn profile, Stack-Overflow or MSDN signatures, and whatever other sites where you think people would benefit from seeing what you are doing.

Writing out what you are doing—and how you are doing it—is the first step to figuring out what it takes to get your ideas across to other people. If you're like me, you'll refine thoughts and concepts, making them better each time, and you'll find what does and doesn't work for you. The best part is realizing what might have been missing in your previous conversations with team members and where you can make improvements.

And you'll have something, outside of your job, that is yours and yours alone.

It's worth it.

Make the Unpopular Call

There will come a time in a meeting when you are called upon to offer your opinion on how to address the problem of the day or some other important topic. There will be a number of people in the room, including some more senior and some in completely different positions than you. Perhaps there will be people from other parts of the organization who have come together to work out this problem. These people have invited you to the table.

The first time you are sitting at this table, I guarantee you this thought will be running through your head: *They must have meant for someone else to be here. There is another* (insert your own name here) *in this company, somewhere. I am definitely not supposed to be here.*

The group will discuss solution alternatives and the debate will rage back and forth for almost an hour. Then someone will throw up their hands and say, "Let's put it to a vote." One by one, they'll go around, asking everyone the same question. As they go around the room, a knot will start to form in your stomach, because the majority of the table will be going with the opposite idea from what you believe to be the correct path.

You will begin to question yourself, what you are doing here and whether you should simply relent and go with the herd.

It's time to remember who you are.

When you're a new developer starting out, this can be scary, daunting and downright unsettling. After all, who are you to offer up some dissenting opinion to all these smart people whom you respect and admire?

Who are you to vote against your manager?

Who are you, indeed?

Some (maybe all) of these people contributed to the decision to hire you. They did so based on that incredible interview when you wowed them with your demos and wrested control of the discussion from them. They hired you because you brought something to the table that they were lacking on their team—a fresh set of ideas and approaches to delivering solutions.

They hired you because you were not one to follow a flock, but one to lead.

They hired you for this job, this job they didn't realize they were interviewing you for at the time.

Who are you, indeed?

Vote the way you want to. Go against the grain, explain why your idea is possible and leave the room knowing you didn't follow the herd.

It won't always go your way, but people will respect your decision to stand on your own feet and they'll know that when push came to shove, you didn't bend or break. And you will still be invited to the table next time, because they need more people like you.

The Hidden Organization Chart

Most organizations have a chart that outlines who reports to whom in the company. Usually when the first human resources person comes into a company, they put this chart together so everyone has an idea of the formal lines of communication.

At this point, people generally go, "Whoa, really? I report to them?"

You might report to someone on paper, but who says you can't talk to other people?

The leaders, the influencers, the wheelers and dealers, whatever level they are at, wherever they work—if you've identified them as being critical to your continued success, go to them, talk to them, get feedback from them, let them know you exist and what you're striving for.

This isn't about making your current manager look bad or uninterested in you. This is about you building the support system you need to lead the Army of One.

What's on paper is a guide; what you need is up to you.

Don't Forget about You

I love to code and will probably be coding until the day I die. (What the quality will be at that point is debatable.)

You might be asked to lead, but they still need your genius development skills to be focused on training the new kids as they come in the door.

When people assume that taking on a leadership role means no longer coding, my response is always the same:

> "Who told you to stop coding?"
> "Who said you couldn't do it anymore?"
> "Did someone ask for your keyboard?"

The only thing stopping you from coding is that fancy new title, "manager."

I've been a manager, a founder, a vice-president and a product manager, and in all of those roles, I've always kept coding, kept learning and kept grinding.

If You're Getting Bored, Change It Up

Early on in my software career, I took a break and became a database administrator (DBA) for a few years. I was terrified that I might be derailing my carefully planned career with this move, but I was bored where I was, and when I realized nothing in the short term was going to change, I took a chance and started at the bottom once again.

It was one of the best professional decisions I ever made. For me, it crystallized the emotion that goes into taking initiative.

Being a DBA forced me to understand database structures, tables, fields, storage types, reporting, and logical and physical designs. It also pushed me to devote time to performance-tuning the work of my peers and trying to figure out why queries took so long to execute and run. I learned the foundation and fundamentals of data architecture and storage, including boring stuff like which type to use and how and when to use them, and sometimes more exciting stuff like replication and index organization (okay—exciting to me).

By the end of that two-year stint, I was reinvigorated and wanted to come back to software development with a renewed drive, not because I hated being a DBA but because I had all these ideas and applications for using that knowledge as a software developer.

Over time, I became the de facto "software database guy" wherever I was, which afforded me some job security but also enabled me to satisfy my data fix going forward.

When I was making this career change, everyone thought that I was crazy and that I would set myself back. In my time as a DBA, I ended up doing more software coding than I would have done otherwise, because I was able to propose new software solutions to that team (as the de facto developer there) while also pushing myself to learn at an accelerated pace to keep my skills sharp.

Don't buy into the hype. Switching careers, whether permanently or for a short fling, will not set you back. It will set you up for what comes next.

‹TL;DR›

Can you give yourself a kick when no one else is giving it to you?

Can you influence change?

It's easy to read about change in a book, fold down some corners and go *check, check, check*. But it's much harder to put into practice.

Whenever I think of initiative, I think of a clip from Howard Stern's *Private Parts* movie. In it, he has just quit a job that was going nowhere and has packed everything up for one last push. He realizes that all this time he's been holding back, letting everyone else tell him what's right, what he needs to do, and how he should act. He decides in that moment that during this next opportunity, this next gig, he has to let it all out. He can't hold back any longer. He can't keep making up excuses for why he's not where he wants to be.

This is your show and you need to stop holding back.

Over the years, I've been asked how I know when a developer is ready to start leading a team or take on a project. Or why someone who has been with company for a short time is getting promoted while someone who's been there longer isn't.

The answer is easy: when you see someone leading the Army of One—knowing what they want, working toward it, not giving up on it and not holding back, leading the way not only for themselves but for others and not because they've been told that they have to—that's when you want to see what they can do with a team.

4

DELIVERY

When you're the new kid on the block, you can have all the drive you want and take initiative for days, but if you can't deliver, you're not going to go very far. People and teams that under-promise and over-deliver are the teams you want to work with.

If you're leading a team, you are still delivering. That doesn't stop. It's what you are delivering that changes, because it's no longer solely code. Now you're delivering results, teamwork and products, not only for you but for every member of your team as well.

You show up every single day, ready to make a difference for your team.

No matter where you are, what product you are building, what maintenance release of an application you are supporting, what grunt work you are taking on, or what language you code in, you *deliver*.

As far as coding goes, this is the most technical section of the book, but it's all code-agnostic (I don't write any code here) and it applies to everything you are doing.

When we think about delivery, we think about three questions. If you take a quick scan of the questions below, you'll see that you've probably been asked two of these questions by people you work with on an ongoing basis, and/or you have asked these questions before of yourself and others. The third question is the question you are never asked, but it is the question you always need to be asking yourself in order to be successful.

1   What's taking so long?
2   Do I know what I am doing?
3   Will I change the model?

‹What's Taking So Long?›

Whether it's directed at you individually or at your team, you will be asked this question over and over again—by everyone you work with who is somehow related to your code.

It's that one question that you will preemptively answer as the person is heading toward your desk. It's at the core of delivery; the best part about things taking too long is that the only equal and opposite reaction is for things to start going more quickly.

What Are You Building and for Whom?

If you are not asking this question of yourself and your team on a daily basis as you strive to ship a release, you are in for a world of hurt during the beginning, middle, and final delivery of your project.

You must always know whom you are writing code for. I made that mistake with my first little presentation application. I thought I was presenting to a group of tech-savvy, upstart business entrepreneurs who'd be drooling over my use of HTML and JavaScript. Turns out I was presenting to a group of upstart business entrepreneurs who would rather hire someone to build the kind of application I wrote and move on with building their businesses.

Knowing who your users are and what they need from you is crucial to your project's success. There is no bigger development failure than when a developer says, "I didn't build it to do that," when the customer is saying that is exactly what they wanted and needed the product to do.

Cue banging your head on the desk.

In that instant, you have failed because you didn't ask the right questions during the development process, didn't do enough demos, didn't validate the requirements with the customer team and on and on. As a result, you and your team have failed.

Sales staff, product managers and customer support personnel interact with customers on a daily, maybe even hourly, basis. You don't, so you need to put your hands (yes, both of them) up in meetings and ask to sit down with customers, to hear their voices and see their faces contort when they look at the user interface you are proposing.

If you never know whom you are writing code for, then you will always be throwing it against the wall to see what sticks. (Hint: it won't always stick.)

Code like a Crazy Person Is Standing Behind You

I can't take credit for this—none whatsoever—but I love it. And you can replace the words *crazy person* with *ax murderer, serial killer, white walker, boogeyman*—whatever keeps you up at night.

Years ago, a colleague and I were having a late-night discussion about code and all those personal little nuances regarding indenting, naming style, brackets, etc. We all have our own preferences. (The pain is real as witnessed on *Silicon Valley*.) We talked about the need for comments and logging, and whether unit tests were worth the effort or was trusting our gut enough. How much effort should we put into naming classes (all the effort)? What amount of commenting should we put in when checking in code and labeling styles? What about when a build breaks? The list was never ending.

It wasn't a heated discussion; we were simply batting ideas back and forth, but the clincher came when my colleague said, "Code like a crazy person is standing behind you and they will trash your computer if you dare check that sloppy code in."

Simple. Clear. To the point.

From that day on, the quality of my work went up exponentially. Something went off in my head that triggered a sense of the team and the people I work with. What we ship together is more important than what I ship alone, and if I'm slowing someone down in completing their work, I'm not helping the team—I'm hurting them and holding them back.

Find Your Learning Hack

Software is not one language (great) and it is constantly evolving (even better).

New languages and frameworks are popping up all the time. It can be stressful to learn each one, understand the benefits of how they come together, and integrate them successfully into your product to make something that is cohesive and not a mishmash of this month's latest fad.

It's the unknown, and the unknown is fraught with stress and anxiety. Both of those emotions have the potential to throw major hiccups into our delivery goals.

Learning hacks are what help you accelerate the time it takes you to learn a new framework or library, understand the basics of it, and determine how to integrate it into your systems so you can move on and get back to doing what matters. You don't want to be the one who spends two weeks trying to figure out all the wrong areas of an SDK and still be nowhere near making it useful simply because the topic was much bigger than you thought and you got stuck going down a rabbit hole. You want to be the person who figures out the basics in a week and comes back with a plan for what needs to be done next.

You don't need to know everything; you do need to know enough to deliver.

Variables: You need to store data somewhere, figure out how they work, and identify the syntax and variants that go along with them. If you don't have variables, you don't have anything.

Conditional Logic: *If* statements, loops, *switch* statements—all that good stuff that lets you control the flow of your application and handle user input.

Data Access: How do you get data? Is it from a text file, database or cloud storage? Is it structured? Is it not? Do you need to learn all of them? How do you run through a result set? How do you do basic CRUD (create, read, update and delete)?

Structure: How do I structure your code? Is it through classes or files? How do you declare functions and pass data into and out of these libraries? At some point, you are going to need to do some encapsulation of code and figure out how best to lay out this beast. How do you communicate to disparate areas?

Platform: These are all the goodies of the platform that you are working with that provide the context for what you are building to. How do you trigger events? What about doing upgrades? Can your code run side by side with older code? (Insert any other question you have here.)

Is this rocket science? No, I don't even think it would be considered basic science.

And that's the point. The moment you are handed the task to learn that new SDK or language, the pressure is on to deliver yesterday and tomorrow.

"You're the guru. You should be able to get onto this quickly."

"You're awesome. You can make it happen."

I have been that developer. You probably have too, and if you haven't, don't worry, your turn is coming. The nerves and anxiety are real; they swell up inside of you in that moment. You sit there looking at this new "thing" while looking at your backlog and wondering how the two will come together. The lone wolf in you kicks in and you start to think about how this can be done, not knowing how.

As I said, it's not rocket science, but this plan, this list, is a method and routine that has helped me calm my nerves and leverage a proven formula for turning the overly complex into a set of simple milestones that removes the emotion from delivery.

It's my learning hack and it gives me a way to figure out what I need to do, so I don't meander mindlessly through an ever-expanding list of properties.

Change some of it or change it all; put your own twist on it and remove what doesn't work for you. But build a hack that you can employ when it happens, so you're ready.

Half of delivery is about being ready for what's coming down the pipe.

What's Your Estimate?

This is the number-one question that you will be asked again and again and again and again by every person you ever work with, for the rest of your career, whether they lead you or code beside you. You will ponder this question on the bus ride to work or while waiting for last night's dinner to heat up.

It will permeate your soul to the point that when your child asks you how long until you are finished raking the leaves, you will start to consider all the variables around garbage bag size, wind resistance and leaf weight (and by this time, they will have walked away).

We already know that nothing takes two minutes, but what we don't know is all the factors that have to be taken into consideration for a developer to answer that one simple question. They might include the following:

> Have I ever worked on this component before?
> What language am I using?
> Do I know this language?
> Is this a hard problem?
> Do I know the platform?
> Do we have requirements?
> Is this a high priority?
> If so, compared to what?
> When does it need to be done?

And this is just the abbreviated list that will be running through your head.

Estimation in software development is a complex task; everyone has a different approach to getting it done. From my experience, I believe a good estimate stems from our own internal levels of familiarity, knowledge, overall understanding of the problem and confidence.

Because we all have different ways of estimating our work, it is imperative that you *never accept someone else's estimate as your own* because even though it's not your estimate, you will be expected to deliver against that number.

FAMILIARITY

Familiarity plays the most critical factor in estimation. Have you worked on this component before? Do you know all the nuances of what it does or doesn't do?

Familiarity is your baseline for estimation, but it's not a factor we often apply.

Take the following real-world scenario. A software manager I used to work with once performed an experiment to prove how important familiarity is to the task of estimation and how far apart he, his manager, and the developer were in there estimates.

The test was simple.

> Ask the developer closest to the task for their estimate.

> Ask the developer's direct manager, who worked on that task "back in the day," for their estimate.

> Ask the manager's manager, who fully understands the problem but has never touched the code for that task, for their estimate.

The results?

> The developer was closest to the target and eventually delivered.
> The manager was way over.
> The manager's manager was way under in his estimate.

You cannot ignore the direct correlation. Familiarity breeds confidence and confidence can never be contained.

KNOWLEDGE

When I say *knowledge*, you might think I mean overall coding knowledge. This is good, but what is just as important is domain knowledge. Domain knowledge is knowledge that surrounds the code itself—the context. "Oh, you are trying to get this client front-end to talk to that back-end service. The problem is that this legacy app has no interface to it." That's knowledge. Or "You can't talk to that application at all, because it would violate these ethical walls that must be adhered to."

Knowledge, whether it's domain or technical, gives you the frame for the work you need to do. It is through our knowledge that we begin to engage in conversations that start like this:

> "I'm pretty sure that is not supported."
> "We'll have to talk to accounting before going forward."
> "We have an agreement in place where we cannot do that."

Knowledge adds another layer to our estimates.

Not understanding the problem when attempting to provide an estimate is the best way to throw your sprint into turmoil before you've even started. If you are struggling to understand the problem, there is only one person you need to talk to—the person experiencing it.

What matters most in estimates is your knowledge of what you are building and for whom.

If you can't get a hold of the customer or the product manager, don't give up and start searching for the next best thing. You want to engage the person experiencing the problem or wanting the feature you are working on.

If you're stuck on what to ask them, here are a few starters:

> "What problem are we trying to solve?"
> "How will this benefit the user?"
> "Why would I want to use this feature?"
> "What value does solving this problem give to our product?"

Don't ever settle for someone saying "It's in the doc" and deferring the conversation until you read the document for the fifth time. Have them explain it and walk you through it. You need to hear it from their lips.

CONFIDENCE

Lastly, we get into how confident you are with everything you have looked at in building your estimate. How familiar are you with that area of code? Do you understand the problem or is it a net new area? How confident are you in delivering this task?

Keep in mind, our goal here is not to throw out bloated estimates. This helps no one, especially you.

As part of estimation, I err on the side of granularity when I lay out my tasks, especially when I have a low level of confidence in what I'm working on. I do this so I can see the work laid out in front of me but also so my manager can easily see where I'm going with my thinking.

Attempting to undertake gargantuan tasks that are very vague in nature can be problematic for a variety of reasons:

1 People can't look at that mammoth task and tell what is to be done. You might be updating the completion rate, but no one knows what you are completing, including you. You are likely to hide behind the numbers in hopes that everything will "work out."

2 Do you truly understand the problem? It's hard to tell because your work says "Solve for X" and you are coding "X" as we speak.

As a leader, when I see big, bloated tasks on a board, an alarm goes off in my head: *They are keeping way more in their heads than is on paper, and this is not going to end well.* By making your tasks more granular, you are able to look at everything in front of you and assess your degree of confidence, perhaps creating a rating for each task or for the work as a whole.

And what does that percentage give you when you present it to your manager?

It shows your level of confidence in your ability to solve the problem, and that's what we're trying to get at.

If you are presenting this estimate to your team or project lead, this should be a signal to them that you are confident in your analysis and that your estimates are going to be close. You didn't simply hem and haw over it, throw a bunch of numbers together and call it an estimate.

For the math junkies out there, our estimation could be represented in mathematical form as follows:

(Familiarity + Knowledge + Understanding of Problem)
x Confidence (Percentage) = Final Estimate

Estimates are about numbers. If you say, "I'm not quite sure what to do, but when I get over there, I'll figure it out," that's an admission that you are struggling with coming up with a number.

No one is trying to nail you to the wall on when and what you'll deliver, but we need an idea. If you have good managers, they'll know when you are only 10 percent confident in your estimate. That's a huge red flag and they'll want to sit down and help you get that number as high as possible before moving on.

That's the kind of leader you will become when people present their estimates to you.

Iterating Toward Sprinting Scrums in an Agile Fashion

Methodologies and patterns are my favorite part of any software discussion. Positions become entrenched, sides are taken, battle lines are drawn and the fight for glory begins not with *what* we are building but *how* we are going to build it.

Agile, UML, Scrum, sprints, iterations, releases, use cases, user stories, Waterfall, Gang of Four, etc.—these are all great tools to solve a variety of problems, some loved more than others. They all have their uses, they all have a component that might work really well at company X, but then, when you move to company Y, they make no sense whatsoever perhaps due to culture, past experiences, external mitigating factors or internal/external regulations.

Still not buying that one methodology will work exactly the same as it will at different company?

Let me put it this way: It's autumn, and you live on a large property with a plethora of deciduous trees. Tens of thousands of leaves hit the ground at the same time every year. Generally, you would pull out your LeafCropper 3000 to blow all those leaves into one location and then you'd bag them. But now it's getting near the end of autumn, there are only a few hundred scattered leaves left around your yard and the weather is calling for it to be super windy. Being the diligent groundskeeper that you are, you want to get this job done today.

Still going to pull out the LeafCropper 3000?

Probably not. It's not the right tool for the job today. Right now, a rake would be better to counteract the wind and not create a greater mess with leaves flying all over the place.

Each methodology in use today has good and bad traits. Don't fall into the trap of blindly following one when it doesn't help you. Take the best of what all these methodologies have to offer, apply what makes sense to your organization, group and team, and create a plan that makes sense for what your team delivers.

Methodologies (and architecture) are tools for us to use to deliver software. They are not what we are trying to deliver.

The Not-So-Perfect Ship

Another aspect of being a part of work that matters is ensuring you are always shipping. Seth Godin preaches that the goal is not to ship bad work all the time but to let the good out, especially when it's not perfect (https://seths.blog/2018/06/shipping-the-work/).

Ship the Not-So-Perfect Ship.

Being on sprint 78 and having never reached production or had a customer use your product are not metrics for success.

Success is shipping betas to your prospective customers, getting their feedback, getting them to buy into your delivery model, and having them sign on as they progress through the trial process.

Software Development Is an Art

I've always disliked the term *programmer*. Programmers take instruction from product managers, who have written the requirements, tasked out the work and laid it all out so the programmers can jump in and start coding. The same applies to the term *software factory* as it implies an assembly line to deliver code with each person doing the same thing over and over and over again but never checking in with one another or throwing their own ideas into the mix.

Phrases like *handing off requirements to the software factory* and *throwing it over the fence* imply two groups doing their share of the workload but never talking to each other. I find these terms and these phrases too narrow and limiting in their views of what our profession has to offer.

Developers take an idea or a problem and come up with a creative solution to it. No matter what the platform or language they choose, they solve problems. If what the developers have proposed fails, they go back to the drawing board and try again and again until they find a solution that works.

Huge difference.

Developers get involved in requirements discussions and customer trips, and they participate in the roles that go beyond the typical software delivery process.

Be the developer who never forgets creativity, not the programmer who is separated from it all.

You Are Only as Good as Your Last Release

Ask any developer about their best release, and they will tell you the weather, date, major version, build and what they were doing when it rolled off the line.

You will always remember and be remembered for the last good release that you shipped. We always remember the latest and the greatest. If it's been many builds since your last great release, it's time to figure out what's wrong, fix it and make what comes off the line next your best last release.

Make every release your last great release.

«Do You Know What You Are Doing?»

This is a tough question that only you can answer. Software isn't easy. If it were easy, everyone would be doing it. The key is for you to be scary-good at what you do, and for that to happen, you need to be prepared for what's coming at you.

Understand What You Are Building On

Knowing *what* you are building on is worth as much as knowing *who* you are building it for.

My first foray into the world of certificates was a disaster.

I had no idea how to provision them, and I didn't realize I needed a thing called a *certificate authority*. To be quite honest, I started installing them here, there and everywhere on the server, hoping (read: praying) that my application would automagically figure out which one was right and do its thing. When nothing happened (literally nothing happened: it was very sad), I took that painful step backward to learn what certificates were, how they worked and how they could help me. By knowing what I was building on, I was able to suggest new features to our product teams around things that we had never considered, like authorization and expiry. Things that would provide value to our customers and partners beyond our application and give them insight into the platform as well. Learn what you are building on, how things do and don't work, and what you can leverage in what you do. What comes from it will raise your game and the game of those around you.

Build for Performance

Best Feeling in the World: Deploying code into production that never falls over or crashes at the most inopportune times (insert your busy season here).

Worst Feeling in the World: Deploying code into production that crashes at the most inopportune times (still insert your busy season here) and with no indication why.

In on-premises development, your performance woes are known only to you, your team, the customer you are deploying to and their users. But in today's cloud environments, the number of people aware of your error can be amplified to exponential levels simply from someone tweeting it to a friend.

From here, the question you need to ask yourself is, *Did I code for that? Did I code for that potential possibility?*

Writing performant code is no longer an add-on to consider after the fact. It is *always* a requirement even when it is not outlined for you. The onus is on you to get it in there and make it happen. If you receive pushback to do this work, you can't give up; the onus is still on you to get it in there and deliver.

Your role is to ensure you are always delivering, in all meanings of the word, not "delivering when my code can handle it" but "delivering all the time."

The sooner you realize performance is a necessity rather than an afterthought, the sooner you'll start to be recognized for churning out truly stellar code that stands the test of time versus code that looks nice in a white paper but falls down when pushed to the limit. Some of my proudest moments as a developer have been when QA was trying to break code I've written. They'd scaled up the user load, throttled the inputs, and added extra devices, and still my code kept on standing, kept on humming and kept on keeping on. Maybe it slowed down to queue up the requests, maybe it took a few more resources than it normally would, but *it never died.*

Don't leave your performance coding till the end of the release. If it's in the last sprint, that sprint will get cut and your product will get pushed out. Product managers can smell completion a mile away and they know when code is ready to ship. Sales managers sold it the moment you branched the code, and they are dying to get it into the hands of the customers who've been waiting oh-so-long for it.

Selling a release "built for performance with no new bells and whistles" is a hard sell, which is why performance can get buried at the bottom of the pile.

Build your performance work early into your projects and start testing earlier. As new features are added, you can continually run those test cases throughout the cycle and validate the results against the baseline when new functionality is added.

Don't be one of those developers who hides from finding out which part of your code performed well and which part failed. Embrace the realization that your code needs more finetuning and cleaning up so it will stand up longer. This is what you are here for.

Not sure how to get started?

Before you hand off that next piece of code to QA, build a little app, a script, a unit test, something that is going to take your code and load test it. (If it's meant for ten current users, test for a hundred.) Then watch what happens. Did 100X work too easily? Great. Mark it up to 1000X, and run it again.

Did your code break or can you ratchet it up some more?

Keep going until you find that breaking point. Once you find it, let everyone know.

Now you have a baseline for tomorrow's development that QA and product management will want to keep.

The best part about writing performant code? Sleeping like a baby.

Don't Get Lost in Design

You can tell where a developer is spending the majority of their time by how they present the problem they are trying to solve. Are they launching into the perfection of their diagram with all of its "future-loaded" capabilities or are they talking about the customer, the requirements, and the problem they are trying to solve?

What we coded when we "knew enough to be dangerous" is some scary code. It makes us shudder to go back and look at it (so we don't). Heck, code I wrote last week, I would write better this week.

Good developers get lost in the design that their solution has to offer; *great* developers get lost in the customer problem and the requirements. They relish the unknowns and know there is no value in putting an insane amount of effort into a design that is going to change and evolve as time goes on. We are not in this to be amazing box diagrammers; we are in this to code and deliver incredible solutions.

Designs are good, designs are needed, but always remember whom and what you are designing for.

If you're still not buying what I'm selling, here's a simple scenario that might help you out.

When you go to your doctor for a prescription for an infection, do they give you double the dose to make sure you don't get sick ever again? Because maybe your body will store that extra-strength dose of antibiotics for later?

When your right leg is broken, do they also put a cast on your left leg "just in case" you decide to ride your bike next week and break it too? Doubtful (I hope). Don't go crazy on the design; go crazy on the problem you are trying to solve.

Who Wants to Be an Architect?

I'm not sure when it happened, but, at some point, becoming an "architect" emerged as the holy grail of aspiration for developers.

By definition, an architect is someone who designs a thing (a structure) to be built, goes through a number of meetings with regulators to get approval on it and then moves on to the next project. Perhaps they do research into what materials to use, but they aren't doing the building themselves.

Some people find the application of this role to software very appealing. I'm not sure why. My love for coding makes me want to work with designs and see them take shape. It's like watching your kid take their first step: "I had some part in that! Go, kid!" I enjoy looking at the before and after of my work, noticing the differences between where I started and where I ended.

If this sounds like I'm being pretty hard on the architect role, I am. I've been in this role and the only way I have ever been able to make it work was if I was still leading, coding and contributing to delivery, not standing on the sidelines critiquing what the team is doing. Over the years, I've seen architects get further and further away from the code until they are talking in sheer abstraction with no connection to the problem the customer needs solved. When asked how and when these designs can be implemented, a flurry of council meetings and submissions must then be enacted for work to begin, when they were never actually required before. Worse yet is the architect's desire to maintain the status quo and avoid the introduction of new frameworks, effectively killing all creativity in the development of any solution.

All architects are not bad and I've had the privilege to work with some truly incredible individuals, but they all shared the same number-one quality—they kept coding and leading.

THE CODING ARCHITECT

Coding architects couldn't care less about the title. They are more concerned with seeing good design translate into great code. They value watching a team struggle through what they designed so they can learn what they should consider next time and where they need to improve. This type of architect is always rocking the boat, introducing new approaches and frameworks into the code to keep things fresh and to ensure the code base does not become unmanageable or un-up-gradeable in the next six months. They want to do more than stay on top of new trends in technology; they want to under-stand them and get their hands dirty playing with them.

Coding architects are the personification of delivery—trying something new, preparing to fail, working with others, leading by example, pushing through the uncomfortable.

If you're going to be an architect, be one who embodies these values.

Your First Customer Call

The first time you are invited to join a customer call will invariably be a last-minute affair.

Your team lead, product owner or perhaps another devel-oper will show up at your desk and ask you to come into a meeting room to discuss with a customer a problem with a piece of code you wrote. This is not about throwing you under the bus; this is about the team needing your expertise.

The customer could be frustrated, angry or furious that they have to be on this call to solve an issue that is yours (not theirs). At some point in the call, the customer might begin ripping apart the work that you put so much blood, sweat and tears into over so many weekends and late nights. It's disheartening, to say the least, but this is your moment to shine as the cool, calm and collected individual who always makes the save.

Here's what you need to remember before you enter the room and before your customer begins to unload on you:

1 *Respect the customer's opinion.* The customer is not always right, but they are entitled to their own opinion of what has happened. Before you start offering up solutions, ensure you understand the problem completely (from their vantage point) and have listened intently to what is bothering them. Read it back to them so everyone is on the same page.

2 *Get the facts* in diagnosing their issue(s). Ask them what they have done. It is very likely they don't know about all the tools, switches and flags hidden within your code. Help them, educate them and find the patterns behind their actions so you know where to go next.

3 *Establish what's next* while on the call. If you realize it's a quick fix, work through it with them then and there. If it's bigger than that, tell them what is going to happen next. Never end the call with "we'll get back to you." That's vague and misleading. Give them cold, hard times and deliverables that you will lead with on the next call. You don't have to know the answer right now, but you do need to inspire confidence about when you and your team will deliver.

Some people dislike the third step because it creates an expectation that something will be delivered.

I know. That's the point.

Always, always remember that once upon a time this customer bought your software for a reason and they want to use it. Their only problem is they can't get it to work and that's where their frustration lies—they have no personal vendetta with you. All they want is for you to bring them to the promised land.

In the situation where there is no quick fix and it is a complete mess of an issue, this will be the hardest news for the customer to take. They most likely have a whole team of people on their end who were promised that your product would be up and running by end of Y and now it's not going to happen until Z.

Be patient, and work through it with them.

Once the call is over, get your team together to discuss the problem, impressing upon them the severity of the issue. Find out what they need to fix the problem and get it for them.

You are the glue between the customer and your team, and you need to keep them together.

Here are a few phrases I have heard that have sent customers up the wall:

> "It wasn't designed to do that, so I'm not sure why you are using it that way."
> "There must be an error on your side; it's not our issue."
> "I think you need to upgrade."

I have never spoken any these words but have heard the customer responses—not good.

There is nothing wrong with offering a customer an upgrade if their issue has been fixed in that release. However, you better make sure that the issue is resolved and nothing from the new upgrade will negatively impact their system. Asking a customer to upgrade when you're just *hoping* it will work will have disastrous consequences. You will find yourself on a call the day after the upgrade with an even angrier customer who has lost all trust in you.

Navigating your first call, and then working with the rest of your team and the customer to get them back on their feet, are incredible first steps toward earning the respect and trust of your customers in your efforts to deliver a solution to them.

The Customer Trip

You have been asked to go visit a customer site.

You are that good.

Congratulations, this is a huge achievement and a sign of trust and faith in your judgment as something more than a developer.

But now you are on the plane wondering what you are going to do. How are you going to fix the customer's problems? Will all the equipment work? How are you going to deal with all the crazy questions from the liaison you need to work with?

These are good questions, but the only thing you need to remind yourself is this: this is not a vacation, and as long as you don't treat it like a vacation, you will do fine.

From the beginning to the end of each day, you should be focused on being the best representative possible for your organization. You could very well be the first and last image that will be emblazoned in their minds of what your organization represents, so it's up to you to make that positive lasting impression.

Arrive prepared, arrive on time and arrive knowing what you're up against (deadlines, training, sales walk-through, etc.).

Do not come back refreshed. You should come back wanting/needing to take a day off because you are exhausted from all the effort you expended in working with your customer.

If you are returning home from a customer trip without having that combined feeling of "I'm tired from giving it my all but jazzed about making some great headway with the customer," then you haven't given the customer your all.

Customer trips are incredible opportunities to own a problem, lead it and see it through to its resolution right in front of someone who is using your product. These trips strengthen the bond of trust with your customer and make it easier to tackle future issues or get them on board as future "nice" trial sites.

‹Will You Change the Model?›

We all have our own approaches to delivery—what works, what doesn't. As the technology landscape changes, so do our methods for delivery and in order to adapt, the model needs to change and subsequently improve for successive iterations.

You don't need a complicated software, process, schedule, tool, or whatever else you think you need to deliver.

You only need to deliver (don't ever forget it).

"We Delivered More When We Were Smaller"

This, right here, is a knife through my heart when I hear it. If there has ever been a statement that has made me want to curl into a ball and hide in the corner, it's this one.

This is the Mortal Kombat version of "Finish him" to any leader who is working day and night to get a growing team to come together, operate as a whole, implement change and keep on delivering.

What bothers me the most about this statement is that it is thrown around as if it means nothing. But to the leader of that team and to the team itself, it's a kick in the gut. The last time I heard it, I remember asking my manager to not say this in front of the team—they didn't need to hear it. Sure, there were problems; sure, we were working our way through difficulties. But we weren't dead, and there was success on the horizon. We simply had to get there, and we were so close that this would have been the killing blow that stopped us before we really got started.

The problem with the statement "we delivered more when we were smaller" isn't that it's wrong. The problem is that it's an unhelpful simplification. Yes, we delivered more when there was less overhead, less process, less structure— fewer roadblocks in the way. But, as you grow, it's normal to have more formal constraints put in place. We can't be cowboys forever. You'll need to address "hit by a bus" syndrome, but don't go overboard on it.

Note: "hit by a bus" syndrome occurs in small companies, fewer than twenty people, in which one person is responsible for a significant amount of work involved in getting a product out the door. Managers start to question what would happen if that person got hit by a bus on the way to work and was no longer able to contribute for the next two or three weeks. What would be the impact to the next release? To compensate, overzealous managers will implement a significant amount of processes to ensure that this one person is no longer the bottleneck should something go wrong, while in effect adding two to three week to the overall delivery—all before the bus has turned the corner.

If you are serious about having this conversation, start with the roadblocks that weren't in place when you were leading and delivering like champs, what has changed and what needs to change.

The statement "we delivered more when we were smaller" is an easy out; what isn't easy is figuring out how to scale, grow and develop your team, which we'll talk more about in the next chapter.

The Whiteboard Life

Software is about creating something from nothing.

That's the definition that should be in the dictionary because it strips away all superfluous pieces around it and breaks it down to its core. When working with a team, there is only one tool you need to foster that creativity: a whiteboard (and the accompanying markers).

It doesn't need to be translucent; it doesn't need to print; it doesn't need to sync with everyone's tablet. It just needs to be on a wall where everyone on your team has access to use it and can see what is on it.

Don't get seduced by technology. This is all you need.

In living this whiteboard life, there are a few rules you must abide by:

1 Anyone can write on the board. (No one owns it.)

2 PLO (Please Leave On) is for goobers. Whiteboards are meant to be marked up and erased. If you want something left on, take a photo or write it down. Someone else is waiting to get in there.

3 Throw out bad markers—they will not "get better" over time.

Want to know which teams in your company are working together? Check out the whiteboard they use. If it's scuffed up with a variety of handwriting styles and it's a mess, it's a collaborative team, working together to deliver.

Whiteboards are core to your delivery; they are the cornerstone of the collaborative efforts of you and your team. The first time you take a marker to write down your thoughts, it's your show and your ideas, and it's the best way to share them with your team. It will spur discussion, arguments, takeout, laughter and eventually a path forward for the team.

It is the cheapest piece of equipment in your office and the most powerful.

Pray for Your Demos to Break

At some point in a demo, your little globe should keep spinning a while longer or a big red stack trace should assert to the screen or the device brick.

Demos are a quick health-check on where we are in the delivery of software. They are not the gold code; they are not the end product to be delivered to the customer.

A demo should never be scheduled three weeks in advance. Schedule them for tomorrow afternoon or the next day but never more than three days from now. If you schedule a demo more than three days out, you and your team will spend the week preparing for the demo, writing a script for what is to be shown, running through it multiple times and becoming obsessed with all facets of its execution. During this time, you will start to ignore the work that needs to be done for this sprint while obsessing over this vaporware that you are creating.

It doesn't matter who the audience is: after delivering a demo, you need to leave the room feeling uncomfortable, maybe a little stressed. A little armpit sweat is a great sign that you have more work to do.

You should *never* leave a demo satisfied and happy.

There is always room for improvement and you need the feedback from whoever you did the demo for. The onus is on you to push people to tell you what is wrong and where you need to improve. You *need* to know what your extended project team is thinking, what bothered them on the last screen and what might have changed with the customer in the meantime.

You need this information like you need to breathe.

You're not there for the pat on the back and the "well done."

If people are zoning out during your demo, stop and wait for them to zone back in.

If you find meetings have become too formal, stop making them a big event. Instead, invite people over to your desk and give them a quick peek at what's coming next, or walk up to their desk and ask them if they have a second to see what's on your screen.

If no one is giving you feedback during these meetings, start asking the questions for them:

> ➢ "What do you like?"
> ➢ "What do you not like?"
> ➢ "What do you feel is missing?"

These are the growth questions; these are the "how do we get better at delivering" questions that are hard to ask and even harder to hear the responses to. Products get better with feedback and failure—not with pats on the back.

Never leave a demo empty-handed.

Be a Build Breaker

I'm not a source-control guru. I know the basic concepts and have used a variety of systems, labels, gets, check-ins, roll-backs (oh, the rollbacks), moves, branches and trunks to navigate my way around most systems.

But what I wish I had known as a developer on my first day was the importance of source control.

If you are starting somewhere with already established processes, the last thing you want is to be the developer who doesn't understand how source control works and is afraid to check in code because it might break a build.

You know this person. They have all the files checked out, all 159 of them. They have only made changes to seven files but are afraid to check them in because they could break the automated builds that happen thereafter.

The entire point of source control and automated builds is for them to validate work you have done and *break* it.

This is why we have rollbacks.

You don't need to do an exhaustive search on build-breaker jokes or give a hat to the person who breaks the build or put stats on a screen that everyone sees: *Last build broken by Greg.* The memes are funny, but they have it all wrong as they try to make good developers feel ashamed for this behavior.

Forget that.

If I break the build, I *want* my picture beside it with me giv-ing the thumbs-up and a crowd cheering wildly behind me. I want this picture posted by my monitor to remind me to keep pushing forward, to keep trying new things and to never settle.

Breaking a build is a great thing to do. Builds should be broken again and again and again. If you are not breaking the build, you're not raising the bar, and if you're not raising the bar, you're giving your customers the same old, same old—which is what they don't want. Don't hold back your team from using that new library because it might break an interface. Break the interface, recompile, check in and hammer that bad boy home.

I love seeing emails with the subject line *I'm going to check in this code, could break a bunch of builds.* Then I know it's on, we're doing something new, we're giving it our all, and sparks are about to start flying. Time to sit back, watch the build and see what happens next.

You have source control to enable the breaking of builds—it's your safety net. Break away and make something happen.

If your code is so tightly woven together that one check-in breaks everything, the problem is probably not within your source control but somewhere else. Good. Now you know where to start fixing your problem.

As I finish writing this, obviously I need to put on my responsibility cap. It is very bad to break the build without telling anyone you are going to break it or to do so when you're leaving at the end of the day for a three-week vacation. That's irresponsible and that should never, ever happen.

But those are two different scenarios. One is trying to spur innovation; the other is abject laziness that would happen regardless of what source control system you have.

Be the build breaker who's always making your product stronger and stronger.

A Word on Technical Debt

If you are new to the wonderful field of software development, you probably have yet to hear about technical debt.

Don't worry, you will.

You might be coding some of it right now.

In software development, it's said that we always, always need to go faster and *if* something goes wrong, we can go back and fix it later. And perhaps when we go back, we can do it the way we really, really, really wanted to do it in the first place.

As you pursue this constantly evolving and elusive goal, you'll hear great phrases like these:

> "We won't forget about it."
> "We'll go back in the next release and fix it."
> "We'll increase the team after this release and put the new people on it."

If we were to use our family doctor analogy again, the scenario might be something like this:

"Your leg is broken. Here's a splint. It might do the job. I'm kind of short on time— crazy day. Come back in six weeks and hopefully it's healed."

Six weeks later...

"Oooh, that does not look good. Yeah, I should have done the cast the first time, but the ER was busy that day and we didn't want to bring anyone else in, and I had this dinner thing to do, so instead I did the splint. Long story short, we're now going to have to reset it, which will be painful (for you, not me), and put on a new cast. It could take another eight weeks before we can remove it."

And, of course, this will cost you more time waiting for it to heal correctly.

The same symptoms apply to software: time, money, pain and frustration.

You'll spend valuable time fixing the problem.

You'll spend money on fixing the problem that you now have to push back up the line or hot feature to the customer, which will now stop delivery on new, more valuable feature development.

You'll be in pain and frustrated from having to go back and do what you should have done in the first place, but now you have other customers who might be using this feature so whatever weirdness you introduced, others might be leveraging it as useful (seriously this happens). So now it's not a simple fix. Now you need to consider upgrade paths, data migration testing, documentation and support.

Everyone agrees technical debt is bad, but we keep incurring it because it's easy to do when we are busy.

No one is immune to writing code that one day creates technical debt, but we can take the ownership to reduce it and make it better—that is on us, all of us.

If you need to, take on good technical debt—features that provide a big return on investment to your product or team— but reduce the amount of bad technical debt that you take on: bugs that keep coming up every month and, over time, become a cobblestone of patches strewn together across your core engine that constantly require hand-holding.

Above all else, own it.

People Ship Products, Not Process

No one ever thanked the process for shipping code (see the section "We Delivered More When Were Smaller" in chapter 4).

When the chips are down in the final release, it's not the process that will come in early or stay late, or that will choose to invest four hours in that last bug that's holding up the build—it's the people.

Is your team struggling with understanding requirements? Build requirement documents so they can understand the problems better. Are they not sure about their design? Schedule design reviews. Do the Scrum meetings not work at 9 a.m. because everyone is in other parts of the world and they're already halfway through their day? Figure out a better way to do it; use technology to help you out.

Do what makes sense for your team.

At the end of a release, make sure you are thanking everyone who contributed to that product getting out the door; they are the ones who made it happen, not the task board.

People ship products. Don't ever forget that and don't let anyone on your team forget it.

What to Do with Estimates

Leaders have a large role in estimation—they get to add them all up!

But the leader's role goes beyond this. They must challenge the numbers as they put all the data together. As they pull everything in from the team, they are the ones who provide the overall assessment for delivery and what they think the team can actually do.

They poke holes and expose flaws in what has been quantified and ask the important questions at hand:

> "Do you really think you can build that REST service from the ground up in three hours?"

> "Have you thought about where errors will be logged to?"

> ➤ "Are you leveraging our existing libraries or building your own?"

> ➤ "Why aren't you leveraging our libraries?"

> ➤ "Did you know that someone over here already wrote some demo code on this feature? Have you checked it out?"

These are the first-tier questions meant to open up the dialog between you and your team as you seek to insulate their failure as much as is legitimately possible and call out laziness where you see it happening. I once had a senior developer tell me that a single task alone would take two hundred hours to resolve (almost twenty-seven days) for work and code that they had been involved in for a number of years. When challenged on this estimate, they coolly replied, "I guarantee it will be done in that time frame."

In reality, it turned out to be a four-day task and a lot of sitting around simply because the leader was afraid to challenge the developer. When it comes to delivery, challenging your team is where you, as a leader, can have greatest impact on how and what they deliver—it's also one of the hardest things to do each and every day, while motivating them to keep bringing their A-game.

‹TL;DR›

The last question I asked at the beginning of this chapter—"Will you change the model?"—is the gauntlet being thrown down for you. Will you find new routes to deliver? Will you always stick to the path or are you brave enough to try other solutions? Will you challenge yourself and those around you to do and be better?

Delivery is at the core of what you do as a developer. What changes, as you grow, is what you are delivering. Initially, it's all code, all the time. Later, it's motivation, inspiration, leading by example and pushing your team to deliver as well, whether that be through their code or in working with customers.

If you're on the right path to delivering, you should be focused on doing work that matters, doing what's needed to enable your team to grow, and, as much as possible, living in the trenches with your team, knowing when to help them over the wall but also knowing when to step back and let them go.

The next chapter goes deep into leadership and brings together everything we have talked about in the chapters on delivery, drive and initiative. With any luck, you've applied it all to being a great coder, but now it's time to discuss leading and coaching your team.

I want to leave you with this last anecdote that came to me as a new manager. I had been coding like mad up until that point and was now asked to lead a team. In the early days, I struggled to get a handle on making sure I could deliver and lead others at the same time. It was a massive struggle, and the first lesson I learned that brought delivery and leadership together is shared below.

Your Day Begins at 5 p.m.

When I was first promoted to manager, I was gobsmacked by how much I still had to deliver on top of now being responsible for everyone on this new team and what they had to deliver.

Coupled with that, I was drowning in the newfound overhead in supporting the team and still being able to deliver.

I'd ask myself:

How am I supposed to get this all done, when the code, the product and the team now need me?

How am I supposed to fix everyone else's goals when I can't even fix my own?

In the end, I started to see a pattern: *My* day would not really begin until later in the day, maybe at 3 p.m. or 4 p.m. but usually around 5 p.m. From there, I could get in a solid two to three hours of coding before going home. As I became better attuned to my new role, I was able to figure out everyone's schedules and what worked best for them, while still giving myself time to do my work. If I had days that I knew were going to be heavy with meetings and process, I wrote them off to keep my frustration with myself at bay.

You might be scoffing at me and thinking, *That is insane. There is no way I'm going to do that and invest that level of effort for what I'm getting paid.* There is nothing wrong with that choice and you will probably become a good manager and continue to be a good leader. But the scary-good leaders that we all want to be—they figure out what their team needs, how to provide support and how to keep delivering. It's not easy. I've done it a few times and succeeded, and other times, I've failed.

The pace doesn't last forever, but that single revelation is what got me started with leading people and figuring out what I needed to do for them to succeed.

5

LEADERSHIP

Drive, initiative and delivery are all rooted in leadership. Everyone loves the idea of leadership; the word alone invokes memories of past leaders whom we learned from or those that we want to emulate.

There are more phrases that have the word *leadership* in them than code I have written:

> ➤ "I have leadership."
> ➤ "I am the leader."
> ➤ "I will lead this."
> ➤ "We need better leadership."
> ➤ "Let's demonstrate leadership.

Leadership is that shiny new object given to us after years of proving ourselves through developing code, through delivering product, through working with a team, through taking the initiative when someone left the company or when we were short-staffed.

All those actions that showcased your drive, initiative and delivery are what have made you stand out as a leader. Not just someone with the potential to be a leader, but a bona fide leader.

Remember the job that you didn't know you were interviewing for?

This is it. This is that job, and if your interviewers didn't know who they needed before, they know now, and that person is you.

Right now, you're on the precipice of becoming not just a great leader but one of those scary-good leaders remembered years later when people are talking about the glory days over a pint. The kind of leader who receives an email out of the blue from someone you worked with years ago, thanking you for how you treated them in a particular situation or asking how you maintained your cool in a tough situation and still treated your team like the number-one priority.

That leader. You.

The odd thing about these leaders, and about you, is that you've been doing it all along. The recent promotion to team lead or manager was a formality for you that other people need but you don't. You've been doing this since grade school.

The questions around leadership are much more introspective; they are not only about how you want to lead but about how you will instill these behaviors in others so they, too, can get to where you are today. How will they follow your path? It's no longer just about you but about your team's growth and success.

1 Who made you?
2 Whom do you report to?
3 Can you give them more than you have?

Your success will come through what they achieve, and their achievements will be led by you.

‹Who Made You?›

We are shaped by the environments we are a part of, and we are polished by the people who surround us, whether we work remotely or in an office. How your current leader operates will in some way influence the type of leader you will become. You have undoubtedly picked up some ideas and initiatives that worked, some that didn't and others you'd like to forget.

If you didn't have the greatest leaders in the world, you might have already determined what kind of leader you are *not* going to be and how you will treat your team based on those experiences.

Good. Write down all the things that make you who you are as a leader and think about them—remember the section "Go Deep, Take Everything" in chapter 3? Now is the time to go deep and put some serious thought into what that looks like for you. If there is emotion in the picture, keep it off your list; it's not going to help you. Once you've written everything down, circle the items you want to be a part of your strategy in leading people and then, with an even bigger marker, circle which ones you are going to avoid at all costs.

This isn't meant to slight the people who came before; it's about getting you to think about the impact they had on your growth and what you have learned as a result. Leadership is 50 percent awareness—being aware of what is going on around you, anticipating fractures in the team, looking back and questioning what you did yesterday, and thinking about how you'll fix tomorrow's problems before they happen. The other 50 percent? Taking action on that awareness.

I've been pretty lucky with all the leaders I've worked with. I've grown my toolbox over the years and also learned which things to leave behind.

Hopefully, I've done the same things for others.

It's as important to know who you are as it is to know your audience and your team.

‹Do You Want to Do This?›

I want you to ask yourself this question before you continue reading. Don't gloss over it, but ask it directly of yourself—*Do I want to lead?*

Yes, I know I said I'd only be asking three questions, but I wanted to lull you into a sense of security and then slap you upside the head with another big question to drive the point home.

Do you want to do this?

It doesn't matter if you want to lead a team of developers, lead a project, lead the design of a new system, whatever.

Do you want to do this?

Do you want to lead?

This question isn't asked enough when leadership positions are offered to people.

Unless your company is making up positions on a daily basis, generally there is some kind of trigger that has precipitated your being offered this new role—someone leaving, a new project, a new product line, someone's absence and so on. You might be a very good leader who has already demonstrated your ability to lead, but positions will not be made for no reason.

Put a different way: Do you care to lead?

Leaders who care, who want to lead an initiative, a project or a team, will succeed. No matter how much they fear failure because of new ideas, poor product launches or missed deadlines, they will still succeed. They will succeed because they care about the team they are leading and they want to see the team grow, they want to turn team members into leaders in their own right, and they want them to exponentially exceed everything that they already are.

They will succeed because they care about leading this team as much as they care about delivering code.

On the flip side, if the position you are being offered is not one that you want, but it "comes with a better paycheck," remember what the real paycheck is (see the section "Finding Your Paycheck" in chapter 2). This is not it. Turning down an opportunity will not be detrimental to your career. Suffice it to say, I did it twice before the right opportunity came along, and I turned out okay.

Either way, be honest with yourself and don't fall into the trap of drinking everyone else's Kool-Aid. Know what you want. There is more than your success riding on this decision.

This Is Going to Hurt

Look, you're going to screw up, and that's okay.

Anyone can lead when there is money in the bank, when your team is synergizing and delivering like it's going out of style, and when you have no threats in front of you.

Anyone can lead when your competition has folded and given up because you are that good, when you have the best and brightest on your team, and when your customers are tripping over themselves to buy your software, and when, no matter which screen you look at, things are humming along, handling the load like it's a walk in the park.

Anyone can lead under those conditions. Anyone can lead that team because the team is a group of leaders that are meshing together and delivering on their own.

What we need is leaders who can lead when the going gets tough, when things get "complicated," when people are leaving and when there isn't enough money to buy coffee. We need leaders who can keep things rolling without drumming up drama to make things worse or forgetting about the team because they are all-consumed by the threats around them.

That leader, the one who can lead during the bad times, that is the leader you want to be.

Note: Ben Horowitz wrote a great book called *The Hard Thing About Hard Things* that hits the nail on the head about leading during stressful times, making tough decisions and still being a great leader who people want to work for. If you want a book that lays bare the hard times, read this one.

Managers Need Not Apply

If you've ever been a software manager or had some other variation on the title, I have some bad news for you.

You were not and are not a manager. The business card and email signature might say *manager* on it, but it's definitely not who you are and definitely not who your team needs you to be.

Managers are a dime a dozen. In all honesty, I think we have too many.

The process for becoming a manager usually starts like this: "Here you go, Greg. Jeff, Suzy, Megan, Mark and Brad all report to you now. Good luck, guys." And then there are some meetings where you talk about the team's objectives, what the expectations for the team are, what your role is. Maybe you grab a drink together afterward.

Leaders don't start their first team meeting in this fashion. (More on this later.)

If you are a full-blown manager, you're focused on delivery and your little corner of the world. This is why I want to drill into you that you are not a manager. What your team needs is not a manager and what we are talking about has little to do with management.

In software, we use *manager* everywhere. If you see me use it in the rest of this chapter, it's because I'm cycling back to my own time when I was a manager. But in those times when I was a manager, a manager was not what my team needed—they needed a leader.

Own It

A month into being a manager, I was single-handedly holding up a release of our product.

I knew it, everyone around me knew it, my wife knew it and my kids knew it. I think even my dog might have known it. It wasn't for lack of trying; it wasn't because of laziness or because I was new to the role. I was working on a tough problem, and it was taking much longer than I had anticipated. There were many early mornings, followed by many more late nights working on a solution that I had proposed, which therefore made me the de facto owner of it. I did not follow my rules of software estimation (in my defense, I had not established them yet), so I had this working against me as well.

The day the email went out informing everyone that we would be late shipping the release, I stared at my screen, wanting that email to disappear and go away forever.

It wouldn't.

You know that feeling in your stomach when your app crashes and people are trying to use it? It's like a sick, twisting motion. No matter what you do, it never gets better. I had that feeling every day as I tried desperately to get this monster to work.

While reading that email, I learned that proposing a solution is a very easy thing to do. Implementing a solution, making it work, taking ownership of it when it goes sideways—those are other tasks entirely.

Own it: Keep your word, be accountable, and don't sweat it if it's not perfect. But do sweat it if it doesn't get there, and then figure out how to get it there.

Leaders own every mistake they make for the simple reason that they know it will make them better leaders and, as a result, it will give their team a path to follow.

You Are the Team Grunt

Did you really think you'd get to work with all those fancy new code libraries and finalize all those new initiatives that are coming down the pipe?

I have some bad news for you.

You might get to do some fun coding or cool prototypes or anything else you can get your hands on, but your goal is to help your team grow, and this is how they are going to do it. While they are working with all these new libraries to develop their solutions, they are going to need someone to insulate them from all that learning failure and get the low-hanging fruit (all those little bugs) before the final push to delivery. These are the bugs no one wants to work on because they are repetitive in nature, they address parts of the engine no one has looked at in the last few years, or—worse (and my absolute favorite)—they have to do with that legacy SDK or API that no one understands because you can't download it anymore. The only way your team is going to be able to hit their deadline and commitments is if you jump in and make it happen.

Your workload query will now read as:

WHERE BUG_TYPE = "grunt"

You are the leader of the team and you need your team focused on the hardest problems, the ones that will deliver the most to your customers. You're leading the team and picking up the slack.

Yes, it's not the latest, greatest and most awesome set of code out there. But this will put you back in the trenches, working side by side with your team—something you're not always able to do—and ensuring that release gets out the door.

No fancy coffee machine or hydro massage can compete with the level of respect being a grunt will get you.

You will have plenty of opportunities to maintain your skill set and stay "current," but this isn't the time for that. This is the time to lead.

You started as a grunt, and you're going to finish as a grunt.

I Need a Big Team to Be Successful

One of the first questions asked by a new manager generally includes some variant of the following: "How many people are on my team?" (Other versions include "How many people do I have reporting to me?" and "How many people do I manage?")

Does your decision to take on the role differ if it is one person or ten?

Will what you can deliver differ if you have eight people versus eleven?

I hope your answer to both of these two questions was no. The number of people on your team does not symbolize what kind of leader you are.

Instead of asking how big your team is, leaders ask these questions:

> "Who am I leading?"
> "Who needs me?"
> "How can I help them?"

With any team, it's not how many people you are working with that matters. What matters most is how often they show up, how often they put their hands up and how often the team is able to ship. In other words, how much drive they have, how much initiative they are willing to take and how much you, as a team, deliver. Be the leader who kicks ass. Once you start to focus on that goal, your only problem is going to be: *How do I turn away all these people who want to join my team?*

Give Them the Respect They Deserve

Respect is not earned; it is given.

You are the linchpin, you know what needs to be done for your team to be a success, and now it's time for you to flip the script.

If you are going into this opportunity with the mind-set that people must *earn* your respect before you give it to them, then you need to circle back to the section "You Are the Linchpin" in chapter 2.

From your team's perspective, they are the ones who have to transition from whoever was leading them before and now place not only their faith but their careers in your hands. There is a substantial amount of patience necessary on both sides to make things work. If you want your team to take a leap with you, to trust your new ideas and approaches, to put their faith in your career objectives for them, you need to show them that you respect them on day one.

The moment you give them your respect is the moment they will start to give respect to you.

And when they give it to you, they will give it to everyone else on the team. And that's when the magic starts to happen.

‹Whom Do You Report to?›

Remember that company organization chart we talked about earlier? It doesn't matter if you're ten people or a hundred, if the chart is on a napkin or in Visio, everyone knows whom they report to. If you are leading a team, all your team members are displayed on that chart, all showing pretty little arrows leading back up to you.

The problem is, the chart is pointing in the wrong direction.

Unpin that chart from your wall and turn it upside down.

Your team is now above you. You report to them first, before anyone else.

The most memorable end-of-year performance review I ever received came from a member of my team. At the time, we were neck-deep on a very visible project where we were failing daily trying to figure things out, not always getting the results we needed. I was feeling burnt out, running around like a chicken with its head cut off, behind on everything. When I sat down to have a review with a member of my team to discuss their performance (which was great), here's what they said to me: "I think you're doing a great job."

Best performance review ever. I've talked about not standing for those pat-on-the-back, "you're doing great" reviews, but this wasn't from my manager. This was from someone I admired and felt lucky to have on my team, someone who I was trying to lead and inspire to do better.

That fueled me for another seven months.

When I look back, that one comment was the foundation for how the culture on our team began. We'll talk about culture soon. Right now, all I want to emphasize is how easy it is to create a team culture. You don't need a PowerPoint deck or handbook; all you need to start is to know whom you are reporting to.

Leadership Never Happens All at Once

You can't snap your fingers and immediately have your team delivering, driving, initiating as a whole without skipping a beat.

We all want that Cobra/Tiger/SWAT team that can be deployed anywhere at a moment's notice, save the day and get out. Maybe someday you'll get there, but if your leadership journey is just starting, it won't be today, because you're not ready for it

Leadership is a tricky balancing act between managing your team and leading them. Some of your initiatives and ideas are going to take days, weeks and maybe even months before they yield success to your team. It doesn't happen overnight, and that's great, because otherwise you'd miss an incredible ride.

Eventually, you'll be recognized for your "overnight" success, when others step back and go, "Oh, when did you guys do this?" But the seeds of that growth were planted weeks before and the gains are only now visible today.

Recognize this not only in yourself but in your team as well.

Don't be your harshest critic—there will be plenty of others to do that work for you.

Can You Be the Glue?

In the final scene of *Gone in 60 Seconds* (brilliant Nicolas Cage car heist movie, and I completely understand if you want to stop reading and go watch it), Cage's character has to steal a Shelby GT500 to save his brother from imminent death. When he delivers the car, it's scuffed up, dirty, a little worse for wear, but it's there, it works, it's solid, it's functional and it's been delivered.

You can deliver the smooth and polished car late or you can deliver the banged-up car on time, a little worse for wear but ready to go. And when I say "car," I mean your team.

There are going to be times when you need to push them to deliver and times you are going to want the polish. Your team isn't going to be able to choose between one or the other; they will need to do both. You will have to be both and you will have to show them how to be both.

Leadership is about identifying the imminent threat and what needs to be done for your team to be successful, and keeping them together while doing it. You are the glue.

The Non-Leadership Approach

We all have different styles of leadership, and there are way too many for me to go into here, especially since lots of them are undocumented and brilliant.

I have worked with a variety of leaders who have vastly different styles from my own, and yet we were equally successful. Don't get hung up on a particular style of leadership or having to follow to a T what worked for someone else. Focus on developing your own approach, cultivated from what hasn't worked for you.

In a non-leadership approach, focus on identifying the bad habits you *don't* want your team to employ, how you will *not* coach or mentor them, and the criteria that you will *not* measure yourself against when looking at your own success/fail ratio.

It's a list of many *don't*s and *will not*s that do the opposite of painting you into a corner. It's the framework that establishes what you *will not* do and becomes the foundation for all other avenues that are open to you.

When we talk about consistency and change, this is what your team is looking for in addition to new ideas and approaches. Their security will be wrapped up in knowing what you *will not* do and how you *will not* treat them. For instance, you will not achieve anything by yelling at someone when a deadline has been missed because the team was implementing a new library that could improve performance for customers on large install bases. When your team knows this *will not* be the end result, this immediately reassures them about how they *will not* be treated.

At the opposite end of the spectrum, when delivery is taking longer than it should, your spidey sense must go into overdrive as you now need to devise the proper strategies for handling this type of eventuality.

How you solve this problem could involve any of the following: setting up isolated branches for these ideas that won't hinder the main release, communicating extended rollouts to large-scale customers, adding more people to work through the unknowns on the new SDKs, etc., etc.

You've selected one way in which you *will not* respond to an issue; now you need to come up with three ways that you *will* use to insulate your team when the situation occurs.

Be consistent in your approach to how you *will not* lead, keeping the door open for whatever experiment works out along the way.

Don't Follow the Leader

> Don't rock the boat.
> Don't ask the hard questions.
> Take no for an answer.
> Don't try to prove them wrong.
> Don't try out new ideas.
> Go along with the popular vote.
> Don't stand up for anything (and the same goes for sitting down).
> Stay in your lane.
> Don't believe that you can be more.

As the saying goes, "Smile more, talk less."

Become the leader who follows everyone around, never making a critical decision, never changing course, never taking a leap and never failing.

I hope this isn't you, but if you need a pick-me-up after trying new ideas and having them fail spectacularly, this is a good reminder of what the opposite of good leadership is.

Build a Team, Not a Product

I've seen teams focused on functions—"we deliver X, Y, and Z"—where their purpose is defined by what components they deliver. This team setup can be quite effective. However, these teams can struggle when a problem is presented to them and they remain silent or say, "Not our area." That's when the leader lowers their head with a deep sigh, realizing the team is only successful if they are doing things they are comfortable with.

Throwing people together to build a product is easy: find some people, give them a spec, execute.

I don't remember all the great teams I've been a part of, but I remember the broken ones. I remember the broken ones because we delivered much less than we could, we put our hands down more often and we didn't rise to the potential that we had within us. If a team of three is delivering against any problem that comes their way and a team of seven can't keep up, there is something wrong with that team of seven.

Remember the interview for the job that no one knew they needed you for? The same criteria exist for your team; you are building the team not for today, but for tomorrow and next year. A great team will always build a great product. Focus on making the team first; everything else will follow.

You Are Never Too Busy

You are about to get busy, very, very busy (and you might already be). There is no other way to say it—you are going to become in demand. People will follow your lead and want to work with you when they see what you and your team bring to the table. From the success you initiate with your team, new opportunities will start to come your and your team's way.

When these opportunities come your way, pick the right ones and take them if they will help your team grow. The only time you should consider rejecting an opportunity is if it begins to eat into the time required for you to do the work of leading your team.

Don't rely on positive messages rooted in yesterday's actions.

> We haven't held any code-review sessions this month, but last month our QA return rates were zero, so maybe we don't need them anymore.

> No one has come to ask me about having a sit-down, so maybe the team doesn't need them anymore.

> We added three new people this quarter, they've been working side by side with the team and no one has raised any issues with me.

These are all false positives and only serve to assuage that voice in your head that is saying, *You need to do this, you need to do this, you need to do this.* If you are busy, your team is busy. If you are feeling pressure, you know to some extent that your team is going to be feeling it as well.

Leading your team is the work that matters. Don't skimp on it.

At the end of each week, you should always be asking yourself:

> *Are we (the team) challenging ourselves?*
> *Are we (the team) on point?*
> *Are there struggles within the team?*
> *What are we not delivering that I need to focus on?*

If, by asking yourself these questions, you realize that new members need more one-on-one time, but the team is overloaded with deliverables, that's your cue to jump in and lead.

If someone is ticking all the delivery boxes but is feeling completely overwhelmed with things at home, that's your cue to jump in and relax the load.

If everyone is going through the motions and "looking good" but not really doing anything, that's your cue to jump in and challenge them to take that grunt work and eliminate it.

You are never too busy for your team.

Multitasking for Leaders

We've established that multitasking is a myth (see the section "The Illusion of Multitasking" in chapter 3). But, as leaders, we sometimes seduce ourselves into thinking we can make it work because now we have a team of people eager and excited to get work done and delivered. This is false. What you really have is a larger list of *haves*, *needs* and *wants* to get done that go beyond what you personally want to accomplish.

The good leaders line up their team to deliver their *haves*, *needs* and *wants* for them.

The scary-good leaders balance the *haves*, *needs* and *wants* of the team with what the leader is expected to have done that week, and from there they grind on what is left. (We go deeper on this in the next section.)

When done correctly, the team is in alignment and they are on the same page. What needs to get done, gets done.

The First Team Meeting

Don't wait to hold your first team meeting when you become the leader of a new team.

The time to do it is now, at the first opportunity when everyone is available. You don't need days, weeks or even hours to prepare for it.

This isn't the meeting where you are introduced as the new lead by someone else in the company. I'm talking about the first meeting of you and your team where they get to hear who you are and interact with you for the first time.

If your position change is announced Monday morning, Monday afternoon is your meeting. If it's Monday afternoon, Tuesday morning works, etc.

Here is your agenda:

1 Who am I and why am I here?
2 What are the plans for the current week?
3 What do you need help with?

If the team is interested in knowing more about you and your accomplishments, keep your LinkedIn profile up-to-date and direct them there; no need to run through it here.

The goal of this meeting is to identify the trajectory for the team, to say where your focus will be this week, and, above all, to find out what fires need putting out that are holding the team back.

That's it; you're done.

You're not walking through all the changes you're going to implement or talking to one person for ten minutes about their problem on a build machine while everyone else loses interest and starts flipping through their phone.

They talk, and you listen and write, not on a laptop or your phone but on pad and paper. Seeing someone physically write down notes sends two distinct messages:

1 This new person cares about what I am saying and they want to remember it.

2 They are not checking their email while I'm talking but actually listening to what I have to say.

With a notepad, you minimize the barriers in front of you as you are not hidden or partially obscured behind a screen.

Two questions.

That's all you need to ask to get the lay of the land, solidify your path and set the commitment with your team as to what happens next.

Outside of your first team meeting, your second goal is to get to know everyone as much as possible, identify what they're working on, how it's going and, more directly, what they need from you. You don't need to take up a meeting room for a week, usher them in like cattle and have long-winded discussions about goals and expectations. These are informal discussions held over a coffee or a hotdog where the focus is on them and what they didn't want to say during that team meeting—and more importantly why.

Learn Who Your Team Is

Learning who your team is, is not a one-day activity. It could take years to pull back the proverbial onion layers and learn who the people on your team are and what motivates them.

Team events are a great way for the team to relax and hang out together, but you will never learn more about the people who are looking to you for leadership than by spending that one-on-one time with them and showing them how valued they are on this team.

Who are the methodical thinkers and the never-come-up-for-air coders?

Who are the presenters and enthusiasts of the group?

Who are the quiet leaders who prefer to work behind the scenes?

Who works better remotely versus being on-site?

Who are your team members, what do they bring to the team, and how will you help them grow?

This is about moving beyond "About us" to "Who we are" and "Where do we want to go?"

And guess what?

People change over time, and, as a result, this will not be a one-time event but a monthly, recurring event to ensure you continually have your finger on the pulse of your team.

How you get this information from each person is what comes next.

One-on-Ones

It wasn't until I'd been leading a team for the better part of six months that I started engaging them in one-on-one discussions. These weren't formal sit-downs. We'd grab a coffee, maybe some lunch, but it was always a one-on-one format, and, once we both agreed on a time, it could never be rescheduled.

Your team's time is equally as important as yours. Did I need to meet with everyone individually when I could meet with them as a group, air any grievances as a group, discuss our problems as a group and align ourselves to what we were working on ... as a group? Yes, I did, because I needed their perspective, their feedback and their thoughts.

The initial results from the first few one-on-one sessions knocked me off my feet. The discussions ranged from working with others, pressure to deliver, growth paths and reviews (among other subjects). Some topics I had planned for; others I hadn't. Some of these topics were ones that we had discussed as a group, but I didn't realize until then that they needed to be explored more deeply one-on-one.

In some cases, the first few meetings were relatively light, with little information being exchanged. We were in and out in fifteen minutes (most likely because I rambled on for ten of them). Still we progressed and still little was said. It wasn't until the third or fourth session that the awkward silences gave way to floodgates being opened. Had I forgone future sessions based on the first few, I never would have learned all I did from them once that foundation of trust had been established.

I might have been responsible for initiating and running the session, but the session was all theirs to run with and do with as they pleased.

Your team will not magically gravitate to your worldview and non-leadership style simply because you put it in front of them. Patience and showing up every day is what will work, and for each person what you bring to them will be different.

The Balancing Act

It is very important—*extremely important*—that you remember that being a leader is about balance. If you go too far in one direction (for instance, all product matter expert or architect or coder), you will fail your team in all the other areas where they need you.

There are no exact numbers for what works for which type of leader in which type of team. Suffice it to say, you must always be focusing on all levels of drive, initiative, delivery and now leadership across all areas of your work.

Depending on the day of the week, what is happening, and where your team is at, a typical day could include all of the following:

Coding: The team still needs you to be contributing to code and, let's be honest, you still want to be contributing to code; remember, you're the team grunt.

Team Onboarding: Getting new members of the team up and running is critical to your team's continued success and cannot be off-loaded to other people.

Product Matter Expert: You are deep in the code, working with the team to build the products, possibly doling out tasks and assignments. You need to know the products the team is building inside and out.

Product Architect: Note that I didn't say *architect of every-thing*. Could be, maybe not, but at the end of the day, you are responsible for the architecture of the area that you are focused on and working with your team on.

Facilitator: Whether you're dealing with QA, product owners, customer support or anything else, you are the facilitator of these internal roles so your team can get things done. You are the bridge to make sure your team is handling the right priorities at the right time. Occasionally, this might make you the gatekeeper as you try to protect your team from too much noise while keeping the lines of communication open.

Coach/Mentor: Every good team has a leader who has their eye on tomorrow. You keep your eye on tomorrow by coaching your team to be better than you are. Coaching and mentoring involves working with the team to ensure things are running smoothly, finding out where they need help, making time for questions, having an eye on future growth and encouraging them when things are going badly.

You might have to do everything on that list in a single day or maybe it will be spread over a week. You might plan out the week hoping to help the team out with coding duties to get that final build out, only to have to switch gears to facilitating and mentoring instead.

If that's where your team needs you, that's where you go.

Team Lead versus Software Manager

Why are we only discussing whether you should be a team lead or a manager now? Shouldn't we have led with this? Yes and no.

Being a team lead is that middle ground between being a developer and a manager; it's best described as being able to drive but not drink (at least in Canada). In my experience, this role has a certain degree of responsibility and some latitude to implement it. Typically, you're doing more coding than, say, your counterpart, the manager.

If you were to randomly select a dozen team lead job descriptions on LinkedIn, and cross-reference those job descriptions with people currently holding those positions, I imagine you would find differences across all of them between what is advertised and what they do.

Translation: team lead is a wide-open position, there for you to make of it what you want. It is your best and greatest opportunity to try new ideas, fail at them, recover and try again.

Many people see a team-lead role as the jumping point to becoming a manager—*I am next in line, nobody can leapfrog me, I have secured my spot, and now all I need to do is hurry up and get waiting.*

Wrong all day, every day.

You can be a brilliant team lead, scary-good at your role. You may know that this is where you want to spend the rest of your career: working with others on complex problems, focusing on the technical architecture, assisting people with deliverables, raising new ideas and initiatives.

Why stop? If you are continually being challenged, keep doing what you do. But you're not waiting for what comes next, you're focusing on the now.

If you think no one can ever leapfrog you, guess what—anyone can leapfrog you. There is no hierarchy that says, *This person didn't go through the team-lead indoctrination to become a manager, they didn't live in those trenches and they can't make that leap until I do.*

Wrong, again.

There is no queue, and there is no first-in-line. There are only two roles, distinct from each other, complementary in what they can deliver, working in unison to create a great team that can do anything.

Team lead, technical lead, manager—they are all incredible opportunities to hone your leadership skills. In the end it doesn't matter what your title is; it matters what you do when you are there. Leave the titles to someone else to figure out.

The Shuttle Test

Imagine a shuttle achieving liftoff, breaking through the atmosphere, orbiting the moon, entering into a perfect descent and making a crisp landing on the earth's surface.

Now take your current team, all facets of it: business analysts, product managers, developers, systems integrators, quality assurance, support, trial specialists, etc.—and imagine them all on one team, standing in an empty hangar.

What kind of shuttle would they build to execute the above scenario?

Would the end product be able to operate as smoothly as that shuttle?

What would they struggle with?

Where would the gaps exist?

Would they give up?

This is all fictional and you aren't meant to spend days on end trying to figure out all the ramifications of what would come to pass. But you should spend twenty minutes figuring out how it would be built, what it would look like and whether it would be able to *at a minimum* satisfy those basic tests.

If not, try to figure out why. If so, how could you do it better?

The goal is to take a scenario, figure out if your team could do it, identify where the gaps in your skills are and work with your team to eliminate those gaps. Better planning, smoother automation, increased scale—you come up with the metrics and, better yet, get your team involved and see what they think.

‹Will You Give Them More Than You Have?›

There is a moment in every leader's journey when they have to decide how much they can give. In that moment, they can see all the variables at play, all the code that needs to be written, all the requirements that are in front of them, all the outcomes that still need to be completed, the effort, the workload, what the team can do and what else is coming their way.

They can see it as a lit-up path in the night, a way to know exactly where they need to go.

And in that moment, they know there is only one decision they have to make.

Can they give the team more than they have?

Do they have the depth, the strength and the reserves to get them to the other side?

There is no going back once the decision has been made.

There is no committee that will review all the information.

It's you, asking yourself that one question and committing yourself to taking that step. There is no halfway; it's all or nothing.

You Can't Lead Everything

As you find your groove and start executing, people will start to come to you for more help.

And why not?

You're killing it, and they want whatever mojo you have to rub off on their project, on their team and, invariably, on them.

So, you take on more.

And more.

And more.

Until you are stretched so thin that you are no longer killing it and have become part of the failure you were once trying to avoid. We all measure success in different ways. In this scenario, when I say that your level of success has dropped, what I mean is that you still could be delivering, but it's definitely not as good as it once was, when it attracted so many people in the first place.

It's okay success, just not the kind of success you want for you and your team.

I blame the people asking you to take on everything. They are greedy and looking for an easy way out. They're thinking, *I'll give it to them* (you) *so I can move on to easier problems.* They know who you are; they know your skill set, your passion, your drive; and they know you won't give up until you get the job done while raising it to the high standards you have become known for.

To end the cycle and protect your team, it'll have to start with you.

You'll have to be the one to realize you can't do it all.

You'll have to be the one to set the team's limits.

You'll have to be the one to decide when is a good time to say no.

Even though you have to make these tough decisions and have these awkward conversations, just remember, this is where you want to be, this is where you've led your team, and if you want to ensure that your team continues to be incredible, you'll have to learn to say no now and again, despite how hard it is.

Identify What Matters Most: Your Team Culture

The next few anecdotes are focused around that all-important subject of team culture—what it is and how to get it. Buzzwords around fit, disruption, and collaboration are appended and prepended in an effort to make culture more than it actually is. The only buzzword you need to know is the word itself—*culture*.

Culture starts with you.

No matter what the rest of the company is doing, your immediate culture will be the result of your team looking to you for vision, direction and guidance. (Remember that lit path?)

This is the fun part; this is where you want to think big and aim high. It doesn't matter if you have a team of ten or two, you have a culture.

You don't need to do some kind of complicated, out-of-control vision session. All you need is a notepad and some ideas. The goal is to write out a quick set of tenets that you'll use as a guide for what you expect from yourselves and each other, how you treat your customers and maybe what the company as a whole should represent. (Remember Google's old "Don't Be Evil"? Simple, to the point.) Keep your tenets simple enough that people can remember them, allowing them to roll off the tongue.

If you're stuck, here are some of my favorite ones that I have come up with over the years and applied to initiatives, teams, projects and products (some of these should look familiar):

> We imagine, we deliver.
> Managers need not apply.
> Nothing takes two minutes.
> Make it simple. Make it stable. Make it sexy.
> Find solutions where you least expect them.
> Release the kraken... sometimes.
> Fall down seven times, stand up eight.

When you have some ideas, throw them up on your whiteboard, invite the team in and jam about which ones work, which ones don't and what they want to add.

If everyone is a little shy at first and not sure how to respond, write the following questions onto the whiteboard, then promptly hand the marker to someone on your team and sit down:

> Who are we?
> What are we about?
> Who do we want to be when we grow up?

You are the launch pad and they are the ignition so don't ever do this in a vacuum. (The one and only culture killer is to let one person run with it and then present it to everyone in a TA-DA! moment.)

If you want to get fancy, get some mugs made with a tenet on each one or print up some T-shirts. Or maybe just print the tenets in majestic midnight-black ink on a simple 8.5 x 11 sheet of paper and affix a copy to everyone's desk.

Adopting a Team Culture

Each time you undertake an activity as a team, whether in small sub-groups or as a whole group, you are building your culture. If you have built your team tenets, you are tweaking your culture as you go, making it better with each iteration of whatever you are doing.

If everyone is continually buying in, knowing they have the freedom to suggest changes, hacks and ideas to what exists, then you have created the most important element of any culture —adoption.

Anyone can come up with a list of tenets for the team to live by, but if after that jam session, the team goes back to their desks and does the same old, same old, they are not buying in to it, not adopting it, not living and breathing it.

If no one is adopting what you have all done, what you've all put into place, it's not a disaster that needs to be burnt to the ground; it's an opportunity to identify where the alignment is off and figure out a way to correct it.

Go back and do it again and reduce the scope, but get everyone back in and always maintain the adoption—that is the key to any culture success.

Growing the Team

If your team culture cannot sustain the addition of new members, then you have a problem.

What you've created isn't a culture but more of a secret cult that new members need a special decoder ring to access.

Your team must grow, and you must grow them—that is your role as their leader. There is no greater test of the sustainability and scale of what you've created than adding new members into your team and seeing how long it takes everyone to tweak, adjust, adopt and keep on keeping on without missing a beat.

To this end, you need to ask the right questions and set yourself up for success when interviewing new hires for your team. We've all seen candidates that wowed everyone during the interview, and less than two weeks later, they were gone in the middle of the night.

It's the return of the interview; this time, you are on the other side of the table.

BE PREPARED

If you want to hire the best, then you need to show them what the best has to offer. In every interview, you should have your list of questions prepped and ready to go, questions that matter to you and your team (getting their contributions here is great way to address any concerns they might have). I'm not talking about questions that have yes/no answers but questions that require pause and thought before they are answered. Open-ended questions. Don't go downloading questions from the internet that every software developer should know. You already know what they need to know to be a part of what you've created.

If they are the candidates you want, they already know what perks they are interested in—your team, not a beanbag or coffee machine.

They want you.

SAY HI

I am horribly guilty of not properly introducing myself when I meet people in interviews for the first time. A switch goes off in my head, and I launch into asking questions and then realize partway through that I forgot to say what I do and then I have to backpedal.

To give myself that necessary kick in the butt, the questions that I ask are accompanied by a quick paragraph on the company, the team, myself, the technologies we use and what kind of developer we are looking for.

I set the stage, lay all the cards on the table. There is nothing to hide. The more they know, the better their answers will be.

LET THEM DRIVE

After you've done your spiel, it's their turn to take the lead, take control and impress you. How they want to do that is up to them, but it's their turn to drive.

You are not responsible for doing all the prompting and probing to get them to answer your questions. They are here for the job that they want, you've laid it out on the table and it's time for them to pick it up.

Some candidates are extremely nervous during interviews, so you might need to do more prodding than you would normally do to get the answers out of them that you need in order to make a decision to move forward. If you see that spark, pull out the question that will get anyone talking:

"Could you walk me through your biggest success?"

A candidate might take a few minutes to pick the best one, but they will pick one, and if it is as good as they think, they will open up about what it was and what their contribution to it was, and the rest will be history.

If the candidate is struggling, throw them a lifeline and ask them to draw it out on the board. We all love whiteboards; whiteboards are our friends and there is no better way to relax a candidate than to have them turn to an old friend for help. While they are drawing it out, interject with questions. With marker in hand, their confidence level will rise and they will answer.

And if you are doing interviews away from a whiteboard... For shame.

Your first insight into the candidate should come when you ask them if there is anything they would change about what they did. If they say yes, great; if they say no, that's a red flag— there is always room for change. Any code you or I have ever written, we've wanted to change. That's why there is a term for it (*refactoring*, but you knew that).

THE FINAL DECISION

It's always a good idea to invite someone from your team into the interview. It doesn't matter what level of coder they are. They are all going to have to work with the new hire. Implementing an interview rotation is an easy way to keep it simple and give everyone an opportunity to test out their interviewing skills.

The rules that you set out for yourself apply to the team as well: come up with your own questions, questions that matter. You have a skilled team of coders in your group; they can come up with questions that rival anything available for download.

You won't be able to involve everyone in the process every time and you are not expected to consult with everyone on the final decision. That rests with you. Take your time. There is no rush. Remember what your team needs and go from there.

Always remember what you are interviewing them for— the position that is not posted, the one they do not know about, the one that you have not even thought about, but the one that is always lingering at the back of your mind. It doesn't have a title yet or a job description, but it's there, waiting to be filled.

It could be taking over for you, leading a new project, developing a new product, going off on some kind of research excursion, but they all require the same skills to be successful. The job hasn't been created yet, but it's the one that matters most.

The Weakest Member on Your Team

It's going to happen.

One day, as you look through all the great successes and experiences of your team, you might start to realize something disconcerting about where you are as a team—on a plateau, where no one is growing and everyone is stabilizing.

Something will be tugging at you, asking you those tough questions:

> *What is holding us back?*
> *Are we weak somewhere?*
> *When did this happen?*

If there is a member of your team who you feel isn't as strong (and this does not mean strong as a coder but in everything else we have discussed), there is only one question you need to be asking yourself: *Am I willing to put in the effort to take them from weak to strong and get my team back to where they should be?*

It's not uncommon for management to show up at your desk one day and say, "We need to trim 10 percent. Who's your bottom performer?"

Your answer should always be, "No one. They are all top performers."

To be able to say this with confidence, you must put in the effort to make sure there never is a weak link.

Treat the Team like Family

As parents, there are days when your kids annoy you to no end, driving you up the wall. When you think you've had it, they do something that makes you swell with pride, leaving you with a foolish grin on your face.

Whether they do right or wrong, whether they need to be told to not do that thing again or congratulated on a job well done, you will not disown them. You love and care for them and have faith that they will one day achieve accomplishments greater than you ever will.

Would you fire your kids if they did that one thing wrong?

You will have to let someone on your team go someday. It's an inevitability; it will happen. If it's a knee-jerk reaction to something they did that angered you, that's not treating your team like your family. If it's something that you believe in your heart of hearts is the right thing to do because they need that tough love and empathy to help them grow and get better, then make that call.

If you treat your family with patience, treat your team that way. If you lead your family by example, do the same thing for your team.

Those Awkward Conversations

We all have different ways of receiving and processing "bad news" that goes against our internal view of ourselves, who we are and what we are about. Someone has come into your world, breaking your frame and imposing their worldview on your perfectly good approach to life.

No matter how well your team is humming along, incidents will pop up where you need to have those awkward conversations with people on your team, where you'll need to dig deep, see what's really going on and act on it.

These conversations are not awkward because you are discussing what happened. You'll both already know. The awkward part will be trying to find the way forward.

In terms of your conduct in these conversations, I've generally found the following rules helpful when talking to others:

1 **Listen:** Let them speak. You have a lot to say, but so will they. You need to sit back and let that air hang, heavy as it might be, to force them to speak up. (They will.) I've been in these conversations where the air hung for ten minutes. When the person started to speak, the floodgates opened.

2 **Push back:** When you are being pushed away, it is very natural for all of us to simply throw up our hands and say, "Okay, if that's what you want, I'm out." This is what they want. This is the easy way out for them and for you, but when you both leave, no one is happy. What they really need is for you to keep pushing them, keep meeting with them and keep working through it. They are coming to you needing a coach, so coach them.

3 **Follow up:** Who wants to follow up on an awkward conversation? You do. You need to, and they need you to. Whatever the conversation is about, you'll both need a break to think and regroup—this is a great idea. Letting it

go beyond a week and then pushing it out because something came up is a horrible idea. You might as well say to them that you don't care. At most, give it three days, and don't let it hang over the weekend.

The hardest part about these awkward conversations is the emotions that get in the way of solving the problem. Having these rules as a form of reference in your mind will help keep you on track and, when things get heated, take the conversation back to a place where you can deal with the issue at hand and not the emotional context surrounding it.

You will screw up these conversations. There will be some *mea culpa*s—that's how you'll get better and how they will, as well.

My only other piece of advice is to remember who you are having the conversation with. You aren't talking to the whole team, the company or yourself; you are talking to a member of your team. Keep the conversation focused on them and don't make comparisons with everyone else.

Feedback Is What They Need

I've touched on this a few times, and now I want to drive this point home.

Do not sit down with someone to discuss their performance review, whether it be monthly, quarterly, semi-annually or yearly, and give them the following feedback:

> ➤ "You're doing great. Keep it up."
> ➤ "I didn't have anything to add to what you wrote. You're perfect."
> ➤ "I wish I could have a hundred of you."

That type of feedback is a cop-out on your part.

We all have room to improve, room to grow, room to get better at everything that we do.

You are leading a great team that is delivering and driving all day, every day. To give them this kind of feedback will throw everything you have worked hard to accomplish into reverse.

If your team has taken the time to write down everything they want feedback on, you owe it to them to come back with plans and suggestions for how they can get there.

Your team is making the effort every day to show up and deliver; now it's your turn to do the same.

Take that time, put in that investment and help them grow.

Get Out of Their Way

If you watch a skilled athlete long enough, you begin to notice patterns in their play: where they move, how they shoot, when they score.

If you are a parent of a child who plays a sport, you'll watch your kid for countless hours as they go out to their practices and games. As you do, you'll start to observe the triggers in their body movements that signal what is about to happen.

Maybe you are late to a game where they are already playing, but as you enter the stadium/rink/field, that trigger will catch your eye and cause you to stop because you know what's about to happen and by the time you sit down, it will be over.

You will get the same vibe running your team. You will pick up on their cues and triggers when they are entering that zone where nothing can stop them and everything is possible.

The only thought you should have in that moment is to step back, leave whatever it was you were going to talk about, cancel that meeting, close the door and get out of their way.

If you trust them to do what's right, they will get it done and get it done way better than you could have ever thought possible. Stopping by every hour to see how it's going and pinging them with questions and requests is only going to hold them back.

Step back and watch the magic—you'll be amazed.

When Someone Leaves Your Team

If you don't feel that stab of sadness or guilt when someone says they are leaving your team, then you have failed to make that person part of your family. When someone tells me they are leaving my team, I always feel that immediate stab right in the feels. It knocks me off my feet and I zone out for the next thirty seconds. Then it passes, and I'm no longer filled with sorrow or guilt at what I could have done better but feel genuinely excited and happy for this person. They've made that tough decision to flee the nest, move on and forge their own path.

Remember, it's not about how far they can grow *on this team* but how far they can grow, period. To this end, growth will require that people leave (or perhaps take your role) and change will happen. If someone on your team has made the decision to leave, let them. It took a lot of strength for them to make the decision; do not force them to make it again.

I only tried to keep someone on my team once, and two minutes into the conversation, I regretted it and switched gears immediately to providing some guidance and advice on what they should do next. If someone is leaving for the right reasons, let them leave. This isn't a blight on your record as a leader. This is a gold star of achievement that you have inspired this person to step up and take the next challenge—to lead and grow. And now you have the opportunity to once again implement change and keep things fresh on your team.

<TL;DR>

The measurements of leadership are still out of whack when it comes to software. We're measured by how much we deliver, how well we deliver and in what span of time we are able to do it. These measurements are fine if we're measuring our own capabilities directly, but leadership as a whole is an indirect measurement based on the combined success of your team that goes beyond delivery metrics.

You are bringing together a set of people from a variety of backgrounds and disciplines and merging them into a cohesive unit that can drive, deliver and initiate as well as you do. Your responsibilities lie in taking the hits for the team, insulating their failures, building them to meet new and exciting challenges that will come their way, promoting their successes, taking on the grunt work and motivating them to succeed more as a whole than they ever could as individuals.

Your foot might be on the pedal, but you're driving from the backseat.

It can be difficult to handle not having that perceived direct control over your success that you were used to when you were coding your brains out day in and day out.

But you'd be wrong in that perception.

To this day, I still talk with members of teams that I led (and those that I was part of). When we see each other, we laugh about all the things we did wrong and how, somehow, we came out a success. We joke about what we should have done, where we should have gone, what we missed and what we got lucky on. I can't recall in any of these impromptu gatherings talking about what our "culture fit" was like, what leadership styles or management methodologies we used or how the process saved us.

Keep it simple, know whom you report to, and show up, even on the bad days, especially on the bad days, because that's when your team is going to need you the most.

6

GROWTH

n each previous chapter, the third question that was asked was rooted in growth and sought to kickstart your push into that behavior.

Drive: Will you stand out?

Initiative: Are you the Army of One?

Delivery: Will you change the model?

Leadership: Can you give them more than you have?

Growth: What are you waiting for?

When you think of the work you do or your team does, what metrics jump out to you?

> How often are they in the office?
> How many bugs originate from code they are writing?
> What are their overall contributions to releases?
> What is their bug return rate from QA?
> How many unit tests do they create with their code?
> How many customer cases do they close?

These are all quantitative metrics that are easy to measure. We have systems that can help us do this; we can churn out a dashboard on who's our best performer simply by refreshing the browser.

But are they good metrics? Do they tell the story of how your team is doing? Do they allow you to have your "finger on the pulse," as you've been yearning for? Do they leave you feeling satisfied with the growth and development of your team?

Do your metrics look like this?

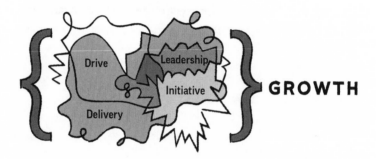

My metrics and your metrics are completely different, but they all lead us to growth.

Growth doesn't come from job title changes, being the boss, focusing on your soft skills, going from junior to intermediate to senior, or even switching companies.

That's progression, it's learning, but it's not growth. It's not the growth we're after.

Growth is what you make of it, and it starts with you deciding *what* you want to make of it.

Want to start a company? Go for it.

Want to be a part of a hugely successful company? Go for it.

Want to volunteer your time at coding competitions? Go for it.

Want to keep doing what you are doing but do it better? Go for it.

Your growth is controlled by you. No one is able to stop your growth except you. The frustration, the confusion, the uncomfortable knot you are feeling in your stomach right now is the realization that you've been letting someone else dictate your growth path; you've been achieving their goals instead of your own.

The goal is to continually keep growing from year one and to not fall back into old habits, to do what you need to do by constantly turning the focus back on you.

1   What's your mark?
2   What value are you creating?
3   What are you waiting for?

‹What's Your Mark?›

Between my first and second jobs, I struggled to find employment (dot com bubble go boom). No one wanted a self-taught learner who had experience building web applications and ecommerce sites but who did not have the paperwork to back it up. Even though I could run laps around other candidates, the measures that were being used to judge me did not align with how I had achieved my goals to date.

I eventually took a job doing source-control management that I hoped would lead me back to the light of software development. My employers anticipated I'd be on the project for a year; in four months, I had finished the project, coded a few other small projects and was back to developing full-time, handing off the source-control admin to someone else.

That was my mark going in: take this project, achieve all its goals, get off of it sooner than expected and get back to doing what will help me grow.

Your mark isn't a score.

It's a line in the sand that you draw today so that when you come back to it three, six, nine, or twelve months from now, you look at it and ask, "How far have I come and how much have I grown?" If you've come a long way in a short time, pat yourself on the back, set your next series of goals and get on them. If you struggled and came up short but still learned some valuable lessons, knowledge and experience, pat yourself on the back, set your next series of goals and get to work.

The measure of your mark is not a plus-one-year-of-experience metric; it's a metric of growth that only you can measure. Others will come to you and say, "Wow, it's amazing what you've accomplished in such a short period of time," and that's great. But that's their measurement for their accomplishments, not yours. Measure yourself.

Our Greatest Failure in Software Teams

Yesterday's unit-test results.

Last week's build breakage.

Last month's horrible patch.

The customer who lost their data.

The server/tenant that went down when resources spiked.

Everything breaks when we push ourselves to become better than we were yesterday. If it didn't break, then it wouldn't be worth working on.

Our greatest failure, however, is when we keep holding on to these "failures," referencing them in meetings when someone suggests a new approach: "Remember how that worked out last time we tried? That's a hard pass. Why go through that again?" We hold on to and use these past failures as justification for not implementing a new change, attempting a new approach. Holding on to these past failures inevitably boxes us in and restricts us from growing.

Those unit tests broke because we slipped in a better performant library and missed an interface.

The build broke because I was trying to decouple our code projects and some older references still exist (in code we don't use anymore).

Last month's update was garbage because the team was pushing so hard to fit that final release for our customers.

The customer lost their data because we were trying to deliver a new upgrade path specifically designed for them.

The server went down because we had not anticipated the spike in demand that was going to come our way and were not ready for it.

These are the success stories we want in our teams. We grow by fixing and addressing these opportunities to make our work better, but we only get there by being able to make mistakes.

Holding on to these "failures" when we are trying to grow serves no other purpose than to force us to uphold the status quo, turning a knob here or a switch there under the guise of growth.

Be the leader who leads growth and change for yourself and your team. Insulate that failure if it's a particularly risky endeavor, but don't stop your team or yourself from making mistakes. Make them, recognize what happened and learn your lesson for next time.

Everything Is an Experiment

We must always have the strength and desire to look back, analyze what went right or wrong, and identify what we can borrow from that experience to get better for the next one.

A good way to think of this is to take every process, idea and suggestion you have and classify it as an experiment. By labeling things in this manner, you shift your paradigm from being concerned about what becomes a success or failure to focusing on finishing the experiment.

What worked?

What didn't?

What do I do differently next time?

When we look at our endeavors as experiments and the results of data, the pressure, stress and concern over success and failure subside as our focus turns toward putting our best effort forward without worrying about any missteps that might occur. Scientists have been doing this for decades; their first try is never their last and they know this when they try the first time.

The rest of us have been slow to catch up.

Getting It Right for One

When the problem is staring you down, it could be that you're trying to serve too many masters. Instead of focusing on getting the entire department trained on the new platform or product while trying to take in all their feedback and make everyone happy, why not focus on one team and a limited set of features?

If the team is still too large, focus on one person.

It could be that it's not the problem that's hurting you—it's your approach to getting it right for everyone.

Get it right for that first person, customer, client, or team member, and then move on to the next and incorporate.

Growth isn't about how many subscribers came online on day one; it's about how many subscribers came from that first user who was blown away by what you delivered on day one.

The Roar of the Crowd

I cannot even fathom what the level of energy from a roaring crowd at any sports event does to an athlete's mind and motivation. Forget a normal regular season game; I'm talking playoffs, finals, the big show.

Now imagine for a second if you had that at work—a crowd cheering you on daily, wherever you were working, for whatever you were doing. Imagine what it would feel like to have an insane crowd, with your favorite colors plastered all over their faces, chanting your name as you compiled that last binary and got ready to push it to production (maybe even untested because, hey, eighteen thousand people believe in you). Or maybe you're finishing that last report where you've put in more effort than you thought possible and don't need to mark it as draft because you already know it is going to be *that* good because you are *that* good.

Imagine that change in dynamic behind you?

But more often the not, the opposite seems true, and it feels like you have a chorus of boos or maybe even just one naysayer screaming the loudest at you, holding you back. You start to think, *I don't know what I'm doing. This is too hard. It's going too slow. I'm failing. I'm messing up. It's going to be late.*

And that's multiplied in intensity when you notice it's 12 a.m. and the status of everyone on your team is set to *offline* or *away* and you're all alone. In those moments, there are no crowds; you have to become your own cheerleader.

You can always pick out the playmakers, the ones who aren't fueled by the crowd but by their own intensity. Their goals don't end with this game or the next; they stretch into next season and beyond. As great as the crowds and fans are, at the end of the last game, they will all go home, and the real players show up the next day to start training for next season when no one is around.

I'll Know It When I See It

No, you won't.

You'll simply have eliminated what you don't want, which you already knew. The only result that comes from this strategy is continued frustration as you and your team try to hit a goal that no one knows exists and it takes that much longer to achieve.

This phrase is an excuse, a smoke screen so people don't have to put in the real work to figure out what "it" is and commit to a path.

A better approach is to take an hour by yourself to think, focus, turn the phone off, stare at that blank whiteboard, eliminate the garbage and bring it down to a few options that would work for you.

Don't fall into the trap of serving people's request for "I'll know it when I see it." Sit with them, narrow it down and pull the information out of them. When you do, you'll both realize what "it" is and know the shorter path to getting "it" done.

The Aftermath of Breaking the Mold

The truth about breaking molds is that after the mold has been broken, when the mold-breaker picks up the pieces and starts putting them back together, it's never perfect. There are jagged edges, cracks and chips everywhere. It works, but it's not perfect.

Breaking the mold is the easy part. Anyone can do that.

Putting the mold back together, looking to the future while also remembering the good points of the previous mold, taking care to fix the leaks and the cracks as the new mold is used and smoothing out the rough spots—now, that is hard. That takes effort, sweat equity and time.

Everyone wants to break the mold, but very few want to put in the effort to craft the new mold afterward.

Change Starts with You

Growth is synonymous with change; you can't grow without changing, and you can't change without growing. The problem with recognizing the symbiotic relationship between growth and change is that we tend to believe that it's not us but others who need to change for us to grow.

Before you can bring change to your team, it will need to be driven by you. You will need to have been living this change for weeks, working out all the kinks for when the team is ready to jump on board and start delivering without skipping a beat. You need to have been living and breathing that change, demonstrating to others how growth can come from change and where it starts.

If you cannot become the change you need your team to be, then you cannot ask your team to lead it for you.

Start at the End

Not with the end in mind, but at the end, when all is done. Start there.

When you've shipped the final build, the last bug has gone out and everyone has gone home.

Start there, at that moment.

Was it worth it?

All the sweat, the long-running meetings, missed opportunities, catch up on new betas, last-minute issues, slipups, team changes, all the struggles you can possibly think of.

Better yet, don't just think about it. Write it down.

Look at that list. Breathe it in.

Ask yourself, *Would I do it again?*

Would I go through that minefield again to get to where I am?

Would I go for another ride at the rodeo or sit it out?

If you would do it again, then this is the path you're meant for, this is what you signed up for and this is what we need you for.

(If you would not, that's okay too. That means you have another path to find.)

The Hidden Truth

Here's the truth: we very much hate measuring ourselves against the hard variables of how we are judged. Salary, bonus structure and titles are simplistic indications of growth and measurement that have been drilled into us since the moment someone asked us, "What do you want to be when you grow up?"

We default to these structures because they are an easy comparison and we don't need to invest time in how we are measured; it magically happens. A couple of LinkedIn updates, people like what we're doing and we are kings and queens.

The hard part comes when we choose the metrics by which we will measure ourselves against others. What I choose and what you choose will be completely different metrics irrespective of our titles. You can be the developer who grows more than your manager, or the team lead who pushes yourself harder than other directors. You can be all these things as long as you're willing to change the measures you apply to yourself (and, as a result, your team).

Find the Metrics That Matter Most

We all have our own metrics that matter most to us, whether we're measuring our own growth or our team's. Even though we know what these metrics are, we struggle because they are more complicated than running some queries that calculate counts and durations.

The following are metrics that should stop and make you think about how you collect data on them and what steps you need to undertake to ensure they are not subjective. They should give you the context to know how your team is changing quarter by quarter, year by year, and help you devise that path for how to get where you want to be.

> How often do the people on your team stand up and volunteer to help out a customer or someone on their immediate team or another team?

> What training did they take this year and what did they get out of it? How much of this training were they empowered to put into practice? Did any of this learning make it to the prototype stage?

> ➤ How often do they challenge the status quo and look to try something else?

> ➤ When did they last suggest a new library or framework to improve on the product? If they haven't done this lately or ever, why not?

> ➤ What goes on when you are not there?

> ➤ How efficient are they at working remotely versus in the office?

The list can go on (I hope it can), yet the purpose is singular in nature. These are difficult metrics you can use to measure the output and growth of your team. Most will be derived observationally; some will involve talking directly with your team and asking them the tough questions that you need answers to.

But measuring the growth and output of you and your team is not meant to be a checkbox or survey results session discussed in the boardroom—it's meant to be much more.

Leaders who start collecting these hard-to-find metrics are the ones who relish the opportunity to challenge and push their team and themselves to grow, knowing the next round of metrics will be that much more satisfying to measure.

‹What's Your Value Proposition?›

If the measurement of growth is seeing how far you have come, then it only stands to reason that knowing where you are currently at is paramount to having that reference point to measure from in the future.

You are more than the code that you wrote on your first day (thankfully), and your value is measured by the drive, delivery, initiative and leadership you put on display, all day, every day, through that code.

In order to properly measure my growth, I began to realize that I, my team and the company I was working for had to be in some form of alignment. Otherwise what I was trying to do for the team might not work for the company and what the company was trying to do might not align with where I wanted to go. In short, if the value propositions of all three were out of sync, the potential for growth would drop significantly.

Your value proposition—the tangible and intangible benefits, the magic, the glue, the gravy, the dedication, the commitment, all those elements (and more)—is what you bring to the table. This goes beyond your job description—realizing what all three need and what you can provide, and finding that opportunity they hired you for.

Many people struggle with their value proposition when they hold that lens up to themselves, their team and their company, only to realize that the alignment is askew. What they are providing and doing is not in alignment with what the team needs and the company wants.

Friction ensues when even one of the three—individual, team, company—is out of alignment with the other two. What the company needs, the team is not delivering, and what the individual wants, the team cannot provide. When this problem is recognized, the leader or those watching may think aloud:

"Yeah, they're great on their own, but give them a team and everything goes astray."

"The company is going in this direction, but they want the team to go in another and won't budge."

"We need them to lead a team and all they want to do is code."

The problem with all of these statements is that they manifest themselves inside of us in the form of confusion and frustration; we feel as if we are not doing enough or no one understands what we are trying to accomplish, and we correlate this to not providing value to ourselves, the team or the company.

It becomes paramount to understand what goes into identifying and recognizing what each one requires.

Your Personal Value Proposition

That innovative spark of magic that you offer in everything you do is a culmination of your drive, initiative, delivery and leadership. You put it all into everything you do—how you deliver code, how you work with your team, how you lead initiatives and how you treat your customers.

This is the source of who you are and what you are able to accomplish. I drew out my growth diagram, but yours could be completely different.

What is it based on?

What factors shaped it?

What led you to where you are today?

What will you focus on most to be a success?

Will you be the technical leader who leads the hard problems?

Will you be the people leader who leads teams and projects?

Will you be the one who goes into a cave with the toughest of customers and comes out on the other side with a solution that will knock their socks off?

Who are you?

Where do you want to go?

When you know the answers to these questions, you will have your core value proposition for who you are, what you do and why you do it. It's the secret sauce that no one else has and that no one else is better at than you.

This is you.

Your Team's Value Proposition

Your value and your team's value can be two wildly different worldviews.

You can't always pick and choose who is going to be on your team; in most cases, members (if not the entire team) will be assigned to you.

Once you have your view of who you are and your own diagram of growth, it's worth the effort to draw out who your team is now and where you want them to go. This exercise can be cathartic as you draw out their jagged edges, polished spots and smooth implementations, and as you answer the questions that spurred you on in finding your own value proposition. Where are they strong? How do they operate? What do they deliver? What are we working toward? What are their goals? Where are we struggling? Take a few passes at putting it together, thinking about what each person brings to the table, where jagged edges and smooth corners exist. When doing this, don't feel as though you need to bring in the team to help. This is your value proposition that you are establishing and it is comprised of three values—yours, your team's and your company's—shaped by your worldview in each case.

(If you do want to do this exercise with the team, have them undertake the process to create their personal value proposition on their own before coming back with everyone, as this will help them understand where they want to go and what has shaped their decisions.)

When thinking about how to construct this diagram, take a moment to think about all that you have accomplished over the past year, where overlaps exist and success and failures have occurred. Don't hold back; put it all in.

The number-one question we are trying to answer at this stage is: Are you and your team headed in the same direction or are you completely disconnected and going off on your own paths?

We are not all the same, nor should we be—remember creativity in software? It comes from different views, backgrounds and approaches to development. What is important is recognizing and understanding these different values so we can determine if they are in alignment.

There are reasons people ask for transfers to different teams or leave companies altogether. The common trope is *people don't leave companies; they leave managers.* This alone is rooted in a misalignment between their personal value proposition and the team's; they can't see a place for themselves in that environment. People leave teams because a new challenge, team, or opportunity exists that better aligns with their value proposition. You won't be able to keep them forever (this is good), but it's up to you to ensure that they are not leaving because they were not on board or felt lost. Instead you want to make sure they've had the type of team experience we all crave and will talk about for years with past, present and future colleagues.

Your Company's Value Proposition

If you are working for a small company (*e.g.*, a startup), what they do and who they are will have a better chance of lining up with your (and subsequently your team's) value proposition. This occurs because the company is small and you can readily see all the moving parts in front of you. You can put your finger on the pulse of the company and get a response with little to no effort, presumably before you even join.

Drawing out the diagram of where the company is focused, where they are headed and what matters to them is a simple task. A larger company, whether they deliver software or the software supports, is an altogether different business; it can become harder to nail down this information as there are a multitude of sources.

What you see as "the company" is up to you. If you want to keep it to your department as a whole because that is where you have potential influence, that is your choice. There is no expectation for you to travel to every regional office to figure out your company's value proposition.

Here are some areas you might want to think about when constructing this diagram as it pertains to your company:

> How do we work with customers?
> How do we communicate with internal teams?
> What do we do when something goes wrong?
> What do we do when something goes right?
> Who do we reach out to when something goes wrong?
> What goals do we want to achieve this year?

All these factors and more are indicative of the value proposition that your company seeks to project into their business.

Putting It All Together

When we place our value propositions together—our own, our team's and our company's—a picture of either alignment or friction starts to emerge. We want to be in a place where all three are closely in sync. We are working together, win or lose. Trust is high, the direction is clear and we are motivated to be there. We wake up in the morning not knowing exactly which precise tasks we will be doing, but we do know that we are working on the right thing and we are doing it in a way that satisfies all three groups.

And how do we realign if they are all out of whack?

Do you jump in and drink the Kool-Aid?

Do you take a step back and try a new strategy with your team?

Do you rage against the machine and take any opportunity to blame others?

The strategies you pick will define what degree of alignment you want. People who are able to align all three will ensure that every customer engagement, every team interaction, every meeting is driven by the core alignment of the three value propositions. Getting it to happen overnight is not easy, but when all three coalesce—your secret sauce, your team's magic, your organization's quick speed to market—then your internal teams, your customers and your partners will start to take notice and know what drives everything you do.

When you look at your own internal value proposition, you have complete control over where you want to go and how you want to get there. With your team, your control is reduced and you become more of an influencer, motivator and leader in an effort to guide that alignment. With the company or department you work for, your role again will change to championing the vision for others to follow. The work is the same, but how you get it done, how you align all three groups, is vastly different.

Growth and your value are not and will never be one-size-fits-all (just as a one-size performance review does not fit each team member the same way).

‹What Are You Waiting For?›

Do you feel as though you're missing out on things by investing in leadership while others are grinding toward delivering the next release? Or vice versa?

Let's recap in case you are.

If it was important, you would be doing it.

If it was critical, you would have already completed it.

If it's being asked for and you don't know how to do it, you're not behind—you're getting started.

Everyone's on a different path, headed in a different direction on a different road.

Don't confuse someone else's path with yours.

You're not missing out on anything; you only think you are.

Growth will not happen overnight; you will not miss out on anything by focusing on what matters to you. Don't get brought down by FOMO (fear of missing out). Keep your eye on the ball and remember what matters most.

Stop thinking about what you might miss and start focusing on what you will gain.

Overnight Leadership

One day you're the developer responsible for your genius level of code; the next day you're responsible for *the team* and dealing with *all the issues* and questions that go along with leading a team.

Success will not come overnight (despite many assuming that it will). You can't turn a ship around on a dime. It doesn't work. It will never work.

Don't put that burden on yourself.

Even more important, don't put that burden on your team.

You Weren't There When That Code Was Written

You weren't there for the late nights.

For the stress-filled mornings.

For the lack of documentation.

For the tight timelines.

For the never-listening customer.

For the demos that had to be delivered.

For the hotfixes and all the patches.

But you're here now, working on it, trying to adapt it, refactor it, fix it and get it up and running once again. The developer who came before you got that not-so-perfect ship out the door because no one else could. Leaders know that this wasn't an individual effort but a late-night team session that made it happen for the team, the company and the customer.

No one will be impressed with how well you can dissect and find problems in another person's code. They will be impressed by what you will contribute to augment it and make it better.

Coaching and Mentoring

When we think of coaches, we immediately go to the sports coach who leads the team to the championships, and when we think of mentors, we immediately go to the wise, venerable master who will point out the error of our ways with a simple poem.

Whether you're leading a team or cranking out code, here's the truth of it.

You are a coach every day.

You are a mentor every day.

You will never know that you were in these roles or what impact you had on these people until they leave your team and thank you for pushing them to the next level. Maybe this won't happen for years.

The goal is not to announce to the world that you are a coach or a mentor but to impart as much as you can on those all around you no matter what role you are in.

Find Your Breakout

Breakouts are the path you take to get from A to B. If you are growing, you are finding the right breakouts to get you there quicker and more effectively than others.

Do you have a breakout strategy for taking that next step in your career?

Do you know where you want to go next?

Do you know who you need help from?

Do you know what you need to get there?

It's not complicated; take a piece of paper and start writing down what you want to accomplish, when, why and where.

Now you have a breakout strategy. It's time to execute.

Shake Up Your Game

Your customers and your team will not be impressed when you rehash the same ideas and approaches from last year's workshop this year. It's easy to do the same thing over and over again because it works. Why rock the boat when things are going smoothly? This is exactly why you should rock the boat. Growth is not smooth. There are always lumps, bumps, twists and turns. Shake it up, all of it. Keep changing, keep pushing, keep trying something new and keep improving and growing.

Otherwise, you risk everyone knowing what you are going to say and doing it before you do it.

Take a Leap

Don't look.

Don't overthink it.

Jump.

Far.

Wide.

Away.

And figure it out when you land.

You'll be okay, I promise, and it will be worth it.

You Can't Teach Confidence

You can nurture it.

You can grow it.

You can lead it by example.

You can demonstrate it.

You can encourage it.

You can motivate it.

You can inspire it.

But you can't teach someone to be confident. You can tell someone today is "confidence day," but it's a process that takes time, and it's not easy. If it were easy, everyone would be doing it.

Whether it's coding or leading, you know what it takes. If someone else doesn't, give them time, support them, encourage them, show them what worked for you and get them there.

And if it's you, put one foot in front of the other and chip away at that mountain.

Refactor the World

Refactoring is no longer just for code.

It's for that last proposal.

It's for your invoicing process.

It's for your leadership skills.

It's for your team's development.

It's for your goals.

It's for your side hustles.

It's for all of it.

Don't make the common mistake and stop at refactoring your code; that is just the beginning.

Find Your Right-Hand Person

No one is going to tell you that you need a right-hand person, especially after you've been promoted into a leadership position with everyone's trust and hope placed in you. But you will need one.

Washington knew all about it (as did Hamilton).

In my first job as a web developer, our lead developer and I went for lunch. We were talking about upcoming projects and some of the initiatives the company wanted to take on. He looked at me and said, "Look, I can't do it all, and I'm going to need someone to know this stuff so we can do what the company needs us to do. Are you that guy?"

"Yes, I am."

Your right-hand person is there to help get you over the mountain, let you be in multiple places when you physically can't be, do the work that matters and lead where you can't. They are someone who can grow with you, zig when you zag, go high when you go low.

And lighten your load.

How to Run a Great Stand-Up

Although stand-ups are a great practice, running them is fraught with many problems.

Stand-ups are not about what is in the queue or what is showing red on the Kanban board. They're about what is coming next and what the team needs to be moving toward.

The leader of a stand-up comes in knowing what people are working on and where they are going next. The value and the questions generated from the stand-up now transition like this:

> "Jeff, I see you've done all your work. Donnie needs help with these tasks to hit our goals."

> "Mary, can you focus on bugs for the rest of the sprint?"

> "Jane, we have this work coming in the next sprint. Can you begin designing that?"

> "Jack, we haven't done much performance testing. Can you queue that up before handing off your code?"

Now that's an example of a successful stand-up that adds value to anyone's day.

They Won't Change so You'll Have to

How many times have you been in a meeting with someone venting about another team member or colleague? I mean venting—ranting, screaming, full-on losing it. Only to have that person end the rant with "This person will never change!"

If they won't change, why can't you?

If you had been expecting this other person to change and conform to your standards, why can't you change and conform to theirs?

Or meet them halfway and show them what change looks like and how it can be achieved?

No one's stopping you.

The Clicking Moment

In anything we do, there is a moment when things click.

It's that final Lego brick that snaps into place so snugly. We didn't have to push and curse for it to fit. It's not too loose and it doesn't fall out every time we touch it.

It clicks.

It's that moment when your code compiles, deploys, turns on and is churning out magic without you having to do anything else.

It's that moment when you've been sick for a week and you come back to the office and discover that the team kept delivering like nothing had happened while also taking the steps to grow and lead on their own.

It's that moment when the master plan you've been working on for so many years comes together and works.

It's those moments you're after, it's those moments that are yours for the taking and it's those moments I hope you will achieve.

‹TL;DR›

No one can stop you. I cannot say it often enough.

(It's why I'm ending with it.)

Whatever path you head down, whether it's code, leadership or something else entirely, you can do it. You can do each of these concurrently; you can embody the dream of coding and leading at the same time.

And you will be great at it.

You can lead through code; you can break the cycle of thinking, *This is it. This is as far as I'll go.* Whether you lead yourself or others, you're a leader. Now that you know, change the game and lead the way.

THE
LAST PAGE

‹Code Your Way Up›

Want to lead that next project?

Code your way up.

Have a problem, but haven't found an app that can fix it?

Code your way up.

Want to work with a team that's always knocking it out of the park but they don't have any openings?

Code your way up.

Not sure what you should be doing, but whatever you are doing is definitely not what you want to be doing now?

Code your way up.

Sound easy? Too good to be true?

It's not easy; it's not a twenty-one-day course that you take to make you a master of all.

It starts with realizing that it's up to you—where you want to go, what you want to achieve, who you want to work with and making it all happen.

And it begins by coding your way up.

‹Acknowledgments›

I started writing this book two years ago.

But I was afraid to publish it, even though I was constantly writing here, there and everywhere. Writing a book was a whole new ball game for me, and it involved pulling everything together and finding the glue to make it all work.

Getting here was not a solo journey.

Thanks to Louise Karch for always believing in me, giving me just the right amount of kicks and putting me in contact with the great people at Page Two. Page Two people are awesome; from the first meeting with Jesse, I felt a wave of relief—this could actually happen.

I'd be very remiss to not give a huge shout out to Seth Godin's altMBA: Prompt 13 was the impetus to write this book. Thank you to the Flax Cohort.

Special thanks to Sarah Harvey, who had to review every word I wrote, multiple times. In her words, I am now the King of Run-On Sentences in her Hall of Heroes (and that probably makes a lot of sense... see, I told you). The first edits were red everywhere... everywhere... but, in the last edit, she stopped me from making changes and questioning myself, quoting my own words back at me.

To the people who read some of my early efforts, sat with me for beers to discuss ideas and didn't let me give up—I thank you. If I was putting together a dream team, you'd all be on it and we'd deliver everything.

While writing this book, I got to reflect on the many, many projects and products I've had the opportunity to be a part of and the people who gave me a chance... and another one... and another one to get it right. I've written some great code and some truly horrific code, but I've also been a part of some truly breathtaking, incredible teams of people who showed me what lightning in a bottle looks like. I don't know if they ever doubted my abilities, but they never showed it.

To the teams I've led, thanks for your patience while I figured it all out.

To Alison and the girls, thank you for giving me the late nights, the early mornings and all the support I could ask for and more to get here—I don't know how you did it.

Oranda For Life.

‹**About the Author**›

Greg Thomas has been a developer, technical lead, architect, product manager, project lead, program manager and vice-president. He has worked with software and teams for the last nine years and continues to ship code as often as he can.

To keep in touch, read, and listen to more of Greg's work go to www.codeyourwayup.com or email directly at codeyourwayup@betarover.com.

Code Your Way Up is Greg's debut book (and not his last).